FROM ALICE
TO BUENA VISTA

FROM ALICE
TO BUENA VISTA

The Films of Wim Wenders

Roger Bromley

Westport, Connecticut
London

Library of Congress Cataloging-in-Publication Data

Bromley, Roger.
   From Alice to Buena Vista : the films of Wim Wenders / Roger Bromley.
     p. cm.
   Includes bibliographical references and index.
   ISBN 0–275–96648–8 (alk. paper)
   1. Wenders, Wim—Criticism and interpretation. I. Title.
   PN1998.3.W46 B76 2001
   791.43′0233′092—dc21   00–058019

British Library Cataloguing in Publication Data is available.

Library of Congress Catalog Card Number: 00–058019
ISBN: 0–275–96648–8

First published in 2001

Praeger Publishers, 88 Post Road West, Westport, CT 06881
An imprint of Greenwood Publishing Group, Inc.
www.praeger.com

Printed in the United States of America

The paper used in this book complies with the
Permanent Paper Standard issued by the National
Information Standards Organization (Z39.48–1984).

10 9 8 7 6 5 4 3 2 1

Copyright Acknowledgment

The author and publisher gratefully acknowledge permission for use of the following
material:

Chapter three is from Bromley, Roger. "Traversing Identity: Home Movies and Road
Movies in Paris, Texas." *Angelaki* 2, no. 1 (November 1995): 101–118. Used by
permission of *Angelaki: Journal of the Theoretical Humanities.*

For Ginny and Michael Bromley, Mary and Gino Zanetti

Contents

Preface

From the early 1970s until the end of the 1980s, the films of Wim Wenders enjoyed considerable success and popularity in Europe, the United States and the United Kingdom. For the most part, the audiences were what have been called "arthouse" rather than mainstream, but *Paris, Texas* (1984) crossed the traditional divide and, with *Kings of the Road* (1976) and *Wings of Desire* (1987), has constituted part of a repertoire of regular screenings of his work. In the 1990s the story was very different because, although the "classic" repertoire still attracted large audiences, *Until the End of the World* (1991) and *Faraway, So Close!* (1993) were both critical and commercial failures. In fact, it took some time for a British distributor to be found for the latter film which did not reach cinemas for several months after release and *Lisbon Story* (1994) was not even distributed in Britain.

Nevertheless, for the National Film Theatre (London) screening of *Faraway, So Close!* which was followed by the *Guardian* interview with Wenders, tickets were extremely hard to obtain and the NFT could have sold twice as many. Similarly, for the NFT showing of the five-hour version of *Until the End of the World* there was virtually a capacity audience. *The End of Violence* was shown at Cannes in May 1997, and was distributed in the UK and US. Wenders also completed another feature, *Trick of the Light*, made with his film students, which had a very limited distribution as it traces a particular moment in early German film exhibition. *The End of Violence* with its critique of gratuitous violence, and an analysis of how people react to violence, renewed critical and mainstream interest in his work. The location in Los Angeles—described by Wenders as a "paranoid city"—also stimulated debate and some controversy. The film did not have the impact of the 1980s productions, but it did achieve wider mainstream exhibition than most of his more recent films. Wenders's most recent feature film, *The Million Dollar Hotel*, which opened the Berlin Film Festival in February 2000 and won the Silver Bear award, received a number of negative reviews and, despite its stars, was only exhibited for a limited period of time. However, at a point when many critics felt that his career was in permanent decline, Wenders directed *The Buena Vista Social Club* (1999) which has proved to be a major international success, voted the most popular film on its UK premiere at the Edinburgh Film Festival in August 1999, and been nominated for a number of awards, including the Golden Globes and the Oscars.

Part of the problem with *Faraway, So Close!* was that people were expecting a sequel to *Wings of Desire* whereas it is a very different film—more accessible, less allusive, and certainly far less filmic. Another problem perhaps lies with the critics themselves and their preconceptions. Geoff Andrews, writing in *Time Out* in June 1994, summarised the critics' "Wenders" very accurately:

From *The Goalkeeper's Fear of the Penalty* through to *Wings of Desire* most of Wenders' work seemed to have its finger firmly on the pulse of a particular contemporary sensibility: that of the vaguely disaffected thirty something male, bemused by the difficulty of relationships with women. Simultaneously obsessed and disenchanted by America and its cultural stranglehold over Western Europe, perplexed as to how to cope with the legacy of Germany's genocidal past, and so rootless as to be almost perpetually on the move. (Andrews, 1994)

Andrews sees the movies he refers to as "homing" in on the "spirit of the age"—mood pieces for white, male, middle-class thirty somethings. Wenders has moved on, but many of the critics haven't. They seem to resent the fact that he has looked beyond their own world to contemplate political change. The jokes, the whimsy, the sheer fun of some of *Faraway, So Close!* have all been subjected to fierce criticism, as has, what has been called, its "surfeit of politics" (the 1980s *zeitgeist* was to be apolitical). Above all, there is a lurking sense that he has lost his sophistication. When, during the *Guardian* interview, he acknowledged that he was now a Christian, there was the proverbial sharp intake of breath from the *sophisticated* audience.

Faraway, So Close! is fairly formless, but this apparent incoherence and drift is appropriate to a sense of living in an "incomplete modernity": it is a reflexive mode of cinema for a post-1989 world which has unmade so many certainties, with no clear directions for imagining/imaging change or renewal. As Wenders says of the angels in the film, they are messengers, not the message—the same is true of the film, it is a messenger. His later work has taken an ethical turn, the narratives have become more affirmative, and the "moral aspect has been transposed from the level of form to the level of content"(Gemünden, 1994: 80). Wenders has said that the images can no longer carry the message. This is something which will be addressed in the final chapter of this book.

Speaking of his 1970s films, Wenders says:

They are movies from a very different world of film-making that doesn't exist any more. Not just for myself, but for anybody else. Seen from today, it's almost like a lost paradise where one could make movies on a different basis. Audiences had a lot more patience and directors had even more patience . . . the whole visual language has changed enormously over the past twenty years. I said once that if I look at my early films now, I get impatient. And I would certainly cut quicker. (*The Independent*, 2 January 1997)

This book is an attempt to trace the development of the principal themes in a number of Wenders's films from the early 1970s up until the end of the twentieth century, trying to situate them throughout in terms of image, gender and narrative and analysing them from a psychoanalytic and political perspective.

A section of Chapter Two was given as a paper for the Ideas in Progress seminar series at Middlesex University; the substance of Chapter Three was published in the journal *Angelaki* in 1995 (volume 2, no.1); and an abbreviated version of Chapter Four was given as a paper at the 1994 BFI European Film and Television Studies Conference: Turbulent Europe—Conflict, Identity and Culture.

Extracts from this book were given as papers at Cheltenham and Gloucester College of Higher Education; The British Film Institute; and the Norwegian Film School, Lillehammer. I should like to thank those who invited me and those who responded to the ideas and arguments made in the presentations. The Broadway Media Centre in Nottingham asked me to introduce the screenings of a number of Wenders's films and I am grateful to the staff there, especially Caroline Hennigan and Laraine Porter, for giving me the opportunity to try out some of the initial ideas for this book.

I have worked at Nottingham Trent University for the past seven years and have benefitted enormously from the presence of a wide range of stimulating and supportive colleagues, including Bob Ashley,

Viv Chadder, Deborah Chambers, Stephen Chan, Mike Featherstone, Sandra Harris, Joanne Hollows, Richard Johnson, Steve Jones, Eleonore Kofman, Ali Mohammadi, Chris Rojek, Ben Taylor, Estella Tincknell, John Tomlinson, Joost van Loon, Patrick Williams and Dave Woods. Thanks are also due to Terry McSwiney who prepared the manuscript with great speed and precision, to Glynis Fry who worked on an earlier draft, to my editor at Greenwood Press, Pamela St.Clair who provided invaluable assistance and considerable forbearance in patiently waiting for the book to appear, and, finally, to Ellen Leiba for seeing it through production. Carl, Catherine and, above all, Anita have cheerfully lived with my obsessions and are always a source of inspiration.

Introduction

The fact that we are living at the turn of a century and at the turn of a millennium has perhaps led us to privilege our contemporary, to claim it as unique and distinctive as a way of responding to the complex, contradictory and shifting phenomena of our time. It could be, however, that we are witnessing a moment in which projects begun in a past contemporary are now reaching completion, or exhaustion. Movements and conflicts begun in earlier times have made displacement and dislocation one of the quintessential experiences of the twentieth century.

Changes in the world since 1989 have re-focused attention on the displaced person, the migrant, the refugee and the stranger—people dispossessed and separated from their identity and their history (not that these can ever be seen as stable or essentialist). This experience needs to be seen in the context of a new global economy criss-crossed by complex, overlapping and disjunctive transnational flows. On the one hand this has led to the deconstruction of existing geopolitical boundaries, to internal crises of coherence and stability, and to the construction of a new social space, at once globalized and local, predicated upon "migrant identity": a fluid becoming in which there is the possibility of developing citizens of a world in which national boundaries are anomalous. So far, this tendency is mainly evident in the realm of the cultural where "border crossing" as a concept is not confined to the literal migrant but has also come to refer to the "borderline" consciousness of already existing inhabitants of a country. This is principally the case in the films of Wim Wenders.

On the other hand, there are those for whom categories of the present have been made unusually unstable or unpredictable, compounded by the presence of refugees, so-called guest workers, and other people seen as being in transition and "not belonging"; in this context, the past has come to acquire a more marked salience, and nostalgia becomes the symptomatic locus of fantasies of identity and belongingness which turn upon origins, roots, hidden histories and shared heritages of language, blood and soil. The former Yugoslavia and the former Soviet Union are only the most obvious examples. In the face of the provisional, the contingent and the transitory, emotional boundaries become essences and ethnic absolutes, and the idea of a nation-state serves as a sentimental myth that offers an illusion of a classless, organic community of which everyone with a particular designation is an equal member, and the "stranger" is rejected, cleansed and expelled beyond the borders of meaningfulness. In a speech given in 1991, "Talking about Germany", Wenders touches upon a number of these issues, pointing out that the "new" country exists "in a gray time, between times, so to speak", and that the residents of a united Germany are not able to define their own country for themselves, or their places in it: "in their blind aggression they are not actually defending territory but rather fighting for inclusion in their own country" (Cook and Gemünden, 1997: 53).

In a context of ethnic absolutism, linguistic militancy and cultural fundamentalism often provoked by the outcome of earlier migrations and the breakdown of complex, and multiple, political formations, it is crucial that the migrant, or "foreigner", should be able to find space to construct an identity that can accommodate what she or he once was and is now supposed to be: an identity that is *somewhere in-between*. This is true also for those who now find themselves actively marginalised or minoritised in societies where they have long been settled. Wenders's films can be seen as "borderline" narratives, texts of "incomplete signification" (and of writers/storytellers, often, with stories which they cannot finish) in which we witness "the turning of boundaries and limits into the in-between spaces through which the meanings of cultural and political authority are negotiated" (Bhabha, 1994: 7). *Hammett* (1982) deals particularly with the problems of "incomplete signification", the fiction-real dialectic and the *made* nature of stories.

The films ask whether identity is to be conceived of as a point of arrival or, more hopefully, as a point of departure. Are we prepared to acknowledge that the in-betweenness of "migrant" identities, in the literal and metaphorical sense, both calls up and calls into question existing referential notions of cultural authenticity and traditional, stable identity? Substitutes, counterfeits, fakes, and proxies proliferate in the films as ways of questioning essentialist and "auratic" notions of the authentic. Can the deeply sedimented and codified social definitions of common sense and rationality be fractured, opened up to their arbitrary nature, and a new viewpoint adopted which offers scope to people moving in and out of borders constructed around coordinates of difference and power?

My work on the nature of belonging has led me to believe that these questions are best posed at the boundaries of nations, cultures, classes, ethnicities, sexualities and genders because this is where the presumption of identity-formation is most put at risk. As borderline/boundary identities—identities at risk—seem to represent a positive, if unsettling, phenomenon by opening up the possibilities of new affiliations, I have chosen to examine a range of cultural texts which raise the issue of what the world looks like from the borderlands. They are, mainly, narratives which give space and voice to the excluded (sometimes self-excluded) and the affectively dispossessed in an attempt to find new ways of responding at a time when conventional and current stories are wearing out. In these cultural border zones, which are always in motion, it may be possible to heal the breakdown in ways of thinking about the future which seems to characterise much of our time. These cinematic narratives will be seen as cultural resources—goods to think with and good to think with. As Don Cupitt says in *What Is a Story?*: "Stories are interpretative resources, models and scenarios through which we make sense of what is happening to us and frame our own action. . . .They shape the process of life" (Cupitt, 1991: ix), a thought which Wenders would echo, except that the issue of "framing" itself is also an integral part of his work: narrative is not an unconflicted process.

The films bring into the foreground, in some instances, the problematic nature of working within "received" visual and narrative currencies. Each narrative is a fictional exploration of the complexities of belonging and identity, the shifting and cross-cutting cultural experience of disorientation and relocation. Neither urban nor rural space is seen uncritically.

Form is a crucial issue because the texts are working against authorised, and authorising, paradigms. They are, frequently, multilingual, polyvocal and varifocal, intertextual and multi-accented. The location of each narrative is a cultural border zone, always in motion, not frozen for inspection: a liminal landscape of changing meanings in which seemingly distinct genders and generations encounter one another's "otherness" and seek to appropriate, accommodate or domesticate it. They operate in narratives "marked by borrowing and lending across [and within] porous national and cultural boundaries that are saturated with inequality, power and domination" (Rosaldo, 1989: 217).

The films are constructed around figures who look in from the outside while looking out from the inside, to the extent that both inside and outside lose their defining contours. Characters smash windows in an effort to breach the gap between inside and outside; stories are repeated in an endeavour to bridge the division between text and its discursive referentiality; photographs are taken in an attempt to close the self/not-self distinction, to overcome the knowledge that "truth", "authenticity" and the "real" are all a matter of representation. It is only with *Until the End of the World* (1991) that a storyteller is able to complete a narrative, and that the issue of image and representation overkill is confronted. The in-between zones (the cusp of inside/outside) are shifting grounds, and displacement and wandering lead to a struggle for space where identity is endlessly constructed and deconstructed across difference. Techniques are used which achieve a certain aesthetic distance, a holding back (there are numerous long shots in the 1970s films, and several strategies by which characters are decentered and detached) but, at the same time, the "inwardness" of violation and displacement is historically framed, although rarely explicitly—until the later films. The narratives are involved in a process of endless locating *and* undermining: belonging is always problematic. All the preexisting belongings and definitions have to be interrogated in order to be *exceeded*.

Each narrative is involved in a process of reclaiming, of travelling back, metaphorically but also literally at times, to an endlessly receding origin or identity which is seen as diacritical and strategical—a strategy for producing a cultural framework for the possibility of *emergence*. Until the later films, however, emergence remains as emergency, or crisis. The narratives are intergenerational and deal constantly with crisis and emergency, as metaphors of the cracks and gaps, the splits and the sunderings, which accompany any return to denied identity or cultural heritage. In fact, the very tracing of the "return", the act of remembering, undermines the very notions of identity or of originary and initial subjectivities. Wenders's 1970s Germany is mappable, its spaces identifiable in a literal sense, but both spaces and characters (nearly all Germans) are inaccessible, or lack access, to a continuous history—hence the endless journeyings.

At one point in *The Location of Culture*, Homi Bhabha uses a particularly salient quotation from Walter Benjamin which speaks precisely to what I am trying to describe: "translation passes through continua of transformation, not abstract ideas of identity and similarity" (Bhabha, 1994: 235). The phrase *continua of transformation*, with its element of untranslatability is an appropriate way of talking about the political conditions of the present, and Wenders's films, I would argue, are attempting to produce analogical cultural forms of this *continua of transformation*, not out of abstractions but from the lived dispersals and survivals of the contemporary which detonate any comfortable idea of the present as a simple continuum. The films engage with and renew/review the past, refiguring it as a contingent in-between space that innovates and interrupts the performance of the present which has cleansed, erased, expelled and buried *difference*, not as a species of exotica or "otherness", but as the indispensable and endlessly renewed condition of the continua of transformation.

Anatole Dauman, the producer of *Wings of Desire*, says that:

At the centre of the Wendersian creation always remains a fascination for the "act of seeing". To see objectively and subjectively. To see from the sky, to see in dreams, to see inside oneself. To see by way of the camera, of a computer, through another person by proxy. What will be the future of seeing? "You can't change the world, but you can still change the images of the world". Wenders said to the Cannes audience when he received the best director's prize for *Wings of Desire* in 1987. (Dauman, 1992: 154)

Seeing through another person by proxy is a feature of many of Wenders's films: each of the figures in *Wrong Movement* (1975) becomes a means of seeing for Wilhelm; the child Alice in *Alice in the Cities* frames a whole series of images of Germany (and of himself) for Philip Winter; the child Raissa's monocular instrument is a metaphor for the re-vision of the principal characters in *Faraway, So Close!* ; in the Keyhole club sequences in *Paris, Texas*, the mirror enables Travis to see Jane (as if for the first time) unseen, while she "looks" in his direction but is unable to see him, only hearing a disembodied voice on a telephone.

In an account of some of the futuristic aspects of *Until the End of the World* Wenders describes the way in which the film is concerned with the evolution of vision: "the actual subject of the film is the act of seeing, consciously, as well as unconsciously, in its oneiric dimension, through dreams" (Dauman, 1992: 163).

In a sense all Wenders's films are about the act of seeing, but in this particular film he conceives of the existence of a cameraman (literally), of someone who "takes" or collects images, "a seer who lends his eyes to those who do not see" (Dauman, 1992:163). In the early films there is a whole range of people who do not see, in a metaphorical sense, including would-be writers like Philip Winter in *Alice in the Cities* and Wilhelm in *Wrong Movement*, Josef Bloch (the name is metonymic) in *The Goalkeeper's Fear of the Penalty* (1972), the frame-maker Jonathan in *American Friend* (1977) and the cinema projector mechanic in *Kings of the Road* (1976).

In *Until the End of the World*, Sam Farber is the proxy seer who uses an advanced video design to capture highly defined images for his blind mother. However, his camera not only registers the "objective" image but also the "subjective" image. Wenders explains that both images are fed into a computer: "both what the cameraman sees and what goes through his mind in that very same moment will be put into the computer" (Dauman, 1992: 166). The precise outcomes of this "double" seeing, including the production of forbidden images and image-addiction, will be examined later in Chapter Four.

As he has often said, Wenders's work is driven throughout by a love of cinema, especially popular cinema, and it is possible (as some critics have done) to see all his films as an extended metaphor of the processes of cinema itself, including what he sees as its distortions and perversions in post-war Germany. The films endlessly quote other films (especially Hollywood movies) and are, both technically and thematically, very self-consciously intertextual. In *The Guardian* interview at the National Film Theatre in London (July 1994) which followed the screening of *Faraway, So Close!* , Wenders remarked wryly that this was not a "filmic" film, apart from references to Hitchcock. He has long tried to generate a syncretic cinema which combines the popular with the arthouse; *Paris, Texas* is probably his major achievement in this respect.

During the interview he talked a lot about seeing (including, briefly, his own near-sightedness) and his wish to take a second *look* at Berlin in *Faraway, So Close!* , rather than simply make a sequel to *Wings of Desire*. Since the earlier film, of course, the Berlin Wall has come down and another, theoretically united, Germany is taking shape. As in all of his films, Wenders emphasised that in *Faraway, So Close!* the camera must be *open*, not blank—passive, but also concerned and emotionally active. Damiel and the child Raissa both look with a unique eye over the city (the opening shot is as if taken from Raissa's monocular eyepiece). The camera, he said, always has an opinion; the pretence of neutrality is an opinionated stance.

The use of angels in *Wings of Desire* and *Faraway, So Close!* he saw as comparable to the role of metaphor in fairy tales, with the camera as a device to translate/decode the angels' "look". In *Faraway, So Close!* , he claimed, the *look* at the world was the subject of the film. For a number of reasons, he argued, the ways in which we see are being transformed, and his recent films have been attempts to bring about changes in ways of looking and seeing, changes which emphasise reflexivity. He spoke of the dangers of an image-saturated culture, of "overdosing" on signs, and argued that films have the capacity, potentially, to "correct" our vision. This is very much the theme of the three films I shall be considering in Chapter Four—revolutionising the angle of vision. As will be seen later, both Rilke and Benjamin are invoked in relation to this.

In an earlier interview (1991), quoted by Lash and Urry in *Economies of Signs and Space*, Wenders talked about the transformations of time and space in postmodernity. As he said at the NFT, *Until the End of the World* is about the restructuring of the gaze, and in the earlier interview he explains:

that our sense of space, our sense of time has in the last twenty years changed. We are travelling differently, we are used to seeing differently, we see much faster. I think that an audience today can apprehend and understand a lot more things at the same time than they could in the past. And also I tried to make a science-fiction film (about future speeding up) because we too can recount (erzahlen) very compressed, very fast and very many things at the same time. (Lash and Urry, 1994: 55)

Until the End of the World not only has this process as one of its themes; it enacts it in the structuring of the narrative and in the cinematography.

In the films of the 1970s, particularly the 'movement' trilogy (*Alice in the Cities,Wrong Movement* and *Kings of the Road*) the travelling is very different; we are aware of *longeuers*, of pauses, of a chrono-logic, of being 'in the course of time' (the German title of *Kings of the Road*), of little lateral activity or simultaneity. The Germany journeyed through is filled with "markers of place" (as Lash and Urry refer to premodern space) but as space to move in and out of, sites and boundaries of memory and forgetting—an *unreflexive*, overaestheticized, "unpeopled", abstract space: the dehistoricised, emptied-out post-Nazi territory, self-absorbed and vacant. All dwelling is contingent, home is a site of loss: the ship, the train, the aeroplane, the car, the mobile home and the road are the only available resources, lines of flight in a masculinist fantasy. Wenders uses the aesthetic resources of cinema to meditate upon the absence of relationships, on nonsignifying symbols, on human distance, and on gendered anxiety. In the later films, the lateral and the simultaneous dominate—time even becomes a character in *Faraway, So Close!*—and the aesthetic is no longer used to reflect upon social processes from a distance. Now the camera enters the film, so to speak, as a resource of "a re-subjectivization of space, only in a reflexive form" (Lash and Urry, 1994: 55). As my later discussion of these films will show, this re-subjectivization is not only aesthetic but has significant political and ethical implications.

In *The Guardian* interview Wenders referred to the earlier films, saying "if I had a story to tell it was a story about men". He added that movies were, of course, nearly always about men, but not with the candour of his 1970s films (this will form the subject of Chapters One and Two). Most of these films certainly feature men without women but not in any positive sense, as these are mainly men in flight from women, as well as from themselves and the unspoken complicity of their parents' generation. Part of the lure of the road is the illusion of individuality and being out of time and history, as well as the relative absence of females. Those that do exist are dumb, framed as stereotypes, murdered, or marginalised into silent, fleeting appearances, except for a few female children, and all without any resources for a "look" of their own. *Paris, Texas* marks a transition to a more prominent role for women—in so far as Jane is, in a sense, *the* subject of the film—and, with Marion's trapeze activity in *Wings of Desire* and a "globalised" Claire in *Until the End of the World*, Wenders has moved to what he describes as "making movies about people now".

This brief book is not intended to be a contribution to the study of Wenders's cinema as such—I am not a film specialist—but is designed to use a number of his films as sources for a cultural understanding of *anamnesis* as "a work of mourning, a refusal to forget the past either by consigning it to oblivion or by making it present (believing that we can fully remember)" (Readings, 1991: 138); to examine forms of masculinity, with reference to the "movement" trilogy of the 1970s and by an extended analysis of *Paris, Texas*; and, finally, to explore the ways in which a restructuring of modes of seeing in the films since 1987 has contributed to the cultural politics and "figural reflexivity"

(Lash and Urry, 1994: 56) of, what has been called, late modernity. Chapter One looks at a range of films from 1974 to 1977 with a particular emphasis on the ways in which post-war Germany is imaged and narrated as a site of loss and amnesia; Chapter Two focuses upon two films where the issue of masculinity is articulated specifically with a larger sense of deep cultural anxiety and fear; Chapter Three is devoted to the film which presents an interface between America and Europe, *Paris, Texas,* and uses an explicitly psychoanalytical approach to discuss issues of gendered violence, home and flight; Chapter Four looks at borderline identities, time-space compression, the role of the stranger, and the post-1989 political/ethical impasse; and Chapter Five considers the direction taken by Wenders's most recent films.

Chapter 1

Lost in Spaces: Through Alice's Looking Glass and a Cowboy in Hamburg

In *Economies of Signs and Space*, Lash and Urry seek to connect "the changing forms of transportation *between* urban areas with the more general debates on the nature of modernity" (Lash and Urry, 1994: 252). They identify the train passenger, car driver and jet plane passenger as emblematic of modernity, with travel as the *modern experience*. *Alice in the Cities*, *Wrong Movement* and *Kings of the Road,* with their mobile, insecure and transient figures, all embody this *modernity*. Another feature of the films is that the figures are decontextualised, with social relations that are, in Giddens's terms, disembedded from the local. Urban space and identity are seen as having to be constantly negotiated. In *The American Friend*, Jonathan Zimmerman (does the name suggest confinement—the room man?) only seems to come alive away from the confines of domestic and work space (he is a frame maker). The two killings he is involved with take place on a subway escalator and a moving trans-Europe express train.

In all of Wenders's films, in fact, landscapes and places are not merely backgrounds or spaces which people simply inhabit, but "are viewed as through a frame" (Lash and Urry, 1994: 255), consumed for their visual quality, as images. In *The American Friend* a film preoccupied with images and image making, a number of technical devices for enhancing and consuming images are introduced at several points in the film. They not only assist in the consumption of images but also demonstrate the illusionist nature of seeing produced by lighting, movement, camera angles and *trompe l'oeil* effects. Robby Muller's distinctive cinematographic signature marks this, and many of

Wenders's other films, with its highly stylised visualisation which changes the scale, perspective, light and space. In a way, the use of sound amplifies the sense of space to produce a distinctively urban Europe of Hamburg, Paris and Munich. These are all intersections—places of change, exchange and interchange—points of arrival and departure in a culture driven by capitalist modernity. The settlements of domesticity and craft work seem alien and anachronistic, the ideological residues of a displaced set of relationships.

Lash and Urry refer to these spaces and landscapes as "visual property" which confer "temporary rights of possession of spaces away from home". For Wenders, this "visual property" was a characteristic of American cinema whose images he consumed, quoted and reproduced throughout the 1970s as a way of gaining temporary rights of possession at a time when European cinema (German cinema in particular) seemed inaccessible. It was only in 1984 that, with *Paris, Texas,* he brought America into European art cinema as more than a source and supply of aesthetic images. This aestheticisation was never merely a matter of tourism for Wenders, however, as the visual property and the temporary rights related to a profound sense of dispossession in postwar Germany, in which even "home" was experienced as a space away from home. Movement in the 1970s films is not flaneurial (as it might be described in *Lisbon Story*, for example) but a symptom of loss, of cultural vacancy. The visual is consumed as a substitute for the evidence of history or the record of memory in a period of cultural erasure. Signs are signs, and images are images, their representational or referential function has atrophied or even subconsciously been evacuated. Philip in *Alice in the Cities* and Tom Ripley in *The American Friend* "bombard" themselves with instant, contextless polaroid images in attempts to arrive at some point of identity, an accessible unit of self-knowledge. The photograph of Alice's grandmother's house is emptied of significance when the current inhabitants have no record or trace of her.

Wenders' figures travel in the "hyper-reality" of post-war Germany, a space riven by all kinds of borders, a place inaccessible and, in Derrida's term, "under erasure". Those traces which remain signify the absence of the marks, not the marks themselves. In a sense, the films are an attempt to invent a set of cultural codes out of the gaps and absences of a motherless and fatherless Germany. For all the restless wandering in these films—the restlessness of a single generation, for the most part, born in the 1940s—there is still a deep longing for belonging. In David Harvey's words: "There is still an insistent urge to look for roots where image streams accelerate and become more and more placeless . . .The forebodings generated out of the sense of social space imploding in upon us . . . translates into a crisis of identity. Who are we and to what space /place do we belong?" (Harvey,1989: 427). Whether it is the photograph of Alice's grandmother's house or the photograph of the vacant lot in *Paris, Texas*, both are examples of what Susan Sontag refers to as a risk-reducing stratagem whereby photography enables people "to take possession of space in which they are insecure. The very activity of taking pictures is soothing and assuages general feelings of disorientation. Unsure of other responses they take a picture" (Sontag, 1979: 9-10).

One of Wenders's earliest feature films, *The Scarlet Letter* (1973) stages the confrontation of Europe with America, locates spaces in which people are deeply insecure and also traces the roots of particular gender conflicts by adapting Nathaniel Hawthorne's 1850 novel. In every way it is a European film which simply has an American setting; even the filming took place entirely in Europe. Although partly shot in an underground studio in Cologne, with the location filming by the sea on the northwest coast of Spain, Wim Wenders's film was an attempt to render Hawthorne's novel in a precise and authentic fashion, although the screenplay was actually adapted from a script by two German writers. The script, interestingly enough, was called "The Lord Bemoans His People in the American Wilderness" which has an Old Testament flavour about it. It also suggests a "chosen" people and a personal God which fits well with the puritan image.

In the process of filming Wenders found the material intractable: "Now apart from the screenplay, the sets and the actors, what reality can you put in a film that's based on a nineteenth century novel with a seventeenth century plot?" (Wenders, 1991: 7) Actually, if he had used the novel more closely and not relied on the original script he may have been able to produce a number of more animated set-pieces which addressed the whole issue of the struggle over "reality" which is at the heart of the text.

Writing in the aftermath of the film's production he attributed its weakness to the restrictive conditions of the filming (the period demands) which, he argued, made emotion impossible. What he overlooked was the dynamic of the reason/emotion conflict, the "disclosed presence" and the repressed spaces of affectivity. At this stage in his career, Wenders was overfocused on the liberal issues of guilt, hypocrisy and individual liberty, and neglected the emotion and reality of a political process, a founding moment in which an exiled community sought to carve out, of what they chose to call a wilderness, a society without ambiguity, paradox or contradiction: a "revealed" polity.

What the film does do well is produce a sense of the spatial parameters of puritanism, its isolation and coastal/wilderness location. There is a strong sense of its minute scale in a continent still in charge of the Native Americans. It is an apollonian community surrounding itself with the stakes of reason against the chthonic and the dionysian— nature and the passions. At the very outset, the distance and apartness of the woman condemned to live outside the community are marked by the camera. The light and the recurring sound of the sea "enter" the symmetries and low-lit interiors of the enclosed society. It is literally, and metaphorically, a forbidding community. The German language heightens its northern European Protestant origins—a space where excess has been banished.

Forbidden to speak in the chapel, forced into subservience lest they seduce men into error, the women in the market place are the most vocal and discordant in their condemnation of Hester Prynne—they only have the space to speak of what they are not, echoing the tyranny of patriarchal literalness. The only woman who bonds with Hester is Mistress Hibbins who lives in the Governor's house (and is an unexplained, ambiguous presence) and manifests signs of mental disturbance. She cries out to Hester to flee to the wilds with her and her "sisters", and is regarded as a witch by the community. Towards the end of the film when the Governor dies and Hibbins is evicted, Hester offers her and her black caregiver/slave shelter in her house. Finally, when Hester and Pearl set sail for England, Hibbins moves to Hester's house, setting a seal on a "sisterly" bond. Hibbins had also identified earlier with Hester by embroidering a scarlet letter on her breast. When Dimmesdale confesses in the meeting house that he is Hester's lover, Hibbins laughs uncontrollably and has to be restrained. In a sense, the film gives her the expressiveness denied to, and by, Hester as she is an analogue and projection of the injustice and hypocrisy of her community's sentence.

When Hibbins is interrogated by Chillingworth, he notes that "blood is running down her legs," and this emphasises the point made earlier about "flows" being inimical to the postural fixities of masculinised puritan discourse. Similarly, when she parades through the settlement in the wig, staff and cloak of male authority she exposes and mocks this postural rigidity; carrying a brand and setting fire to herself on the scaffold is an act of "power mimesis" which appropriates to herself the customary juridical rights of the patriarch. In the novel, Hibbins is an elderly woman, a magnificently arrayed creature of the wilderness and principal actor in all the works of necromancy. In this film she is portrayed as a young and beautiful woman, not unlike Hester physically.

In many respects, the film follows the narrative trajectory of the novel. A clear picture is given of the public and exposed/disclosed nature of Hester's situation through a number of set-pieces. The cinematography is very "painterly", with canvas-like textures, low-lit interiors, sharply etched landscape shots, and with a Holbein-like quality to the movement and faces. The sense of a confined and morally restrictive community, inward looking and insecure, by use of close-up and two shot techniques, is well conveyed, but the film is weakened by the absence of tension and the undramatic, low-key nature of the principal relationships. Having dressed the characters, located the physical and cultural milieu, and composed the shots, there is a lack of narrative momentum and an absence of animation. It relies too heavily on the subtleties of the novel which are taken for granted, neglecting to develop a sufficiently nuanced film with its own explicit rationale and cinematic/image logic. There is a stilted and immobile effect, a sense of animated paintings. The visual "look" dominates. Characters seem merely to be fulfilling roles in a stylised and tableau-like fashion.

One of the strengths of the film is the representation of Pearl, seen by the community and her peers as a witch, but moving independently in and out of the society elaborately dressed in bright colours which illuminate and throw into relief the monochromes of the Puritans. Gnomic, wild, a free spirit, she is the one figure of activity, the child of light, colour and space.

It could be argued that in a society where passion is associated with sin, nature and the wilderness, the passionless quality of the acting is appropriate, but there is (except for Hibbins) little sense of buried, repressed emotion, or of a conflicted, threatened settlement. The power over Dimmesdale which Chillingworth gradually assumes is not explored, nor is there any real sense of the former's "soul sickness" or of the anguished battle between his public persona and his private knowledge and guilt. Above all, the film lacks any sense of depth or interiority. It is conflated and truncated. No sense is given of a culture in which Satan was a living presence, temptation a continuous threat. It is hard to imagine how Pearl was produced from the characters of Hester Prynne and Dimmesdale. We are told that Chillingworth underwent a traumatic experience in the wilderness but, apart from his references to the Native Americans being more humane and less "savage" than the supposedly civilized puritans, there is little evidence of this. The silent Native American who accompanies him seems to have no function other than that he is in the original novel. The "translation" is too literal, decontextualising and monological. The novel's carefully staged sequences, slow, reflective and deliberate—especially Dimmesdale's revelation—are all compressed, "unmarked", and dramatically flattened by a lack of point or direction. The ironies are muted and deflected by the routine nature of the interactions. Although more than half of the chapters in the novel do have a certain static quality, they are informed by the inextricable reciprocity of the characters and the community.

The film makes two significant changes to the novel's ending. Hester and Pearl leave the community by ship. Their leaving is intercut with scenes of Dimmesdale's dying, eventually at the hands of the new governor. Unable to deal publicly with the "sin" of the man whose presence has seemed to be an embodiment of puritan sanctity (the logic of its claim to be an "elect" people), the Governor chokes Dimmesdale to death. By this action, he transfers to the private sphere *directly* what this public power would have enacted ritually and *indirectly* on the scaffold in the market place. It is a strategic homicide to protect the community from its own public gaze, so to speak. It could not bear to look at its own scarlet letter. In the novel, Hester and Pearl remain in the community (although the latter leaves eventually), sharpening by their virtue the contradictions of a "besieged" community. In the novel, Chillingworth remains but dies within a year of Dimmesdale; in the film, he watches Hester and Pearl leave the shore, turns away, sheds his puritan coat, and departs with his Native American companion.

Through Alice's Looking Glass

The child who played the figure of Pearl in *The Scarlet Letter* appears as the eponymous Alice in Wenders's next film. Both adult and child in *Alice in the Cities* (1974) invest the photograph of the grandmother's house (referred to above) with representational qualities, using it as a means of finding a "real", separate from themselves and from the mode of representation itself. For both, and for different reasons, the photograph becomes a stratagem.

In Paul Joyce's television documentary, "Motion and Emotion: The Films of Wim Wenders" (1989), Wenders refers to the early 1970s in which women were making films about women for the first time, and his feeling that it was time to make films about men, but differently (a similar point to the one made in the *Guardian* interview referred to earlier). *Alice in the Cities* is one of a series of films made in the 1970s about men and, in particular, about masculinity as a form of emotional illiteracy.

The film opens with Philip Winter, in New York, taking a photograph of his location with a Polaroid camera; meanwhile, we are taken alongside him as he views a space—a boardwalk—in which he feels insecure and disorientated. He continues to produce a whole string of Polaroids as he focuses upon a lifeguard post, with its possibilities of rescue. He moves away and drives through the familiar iconography of the U.S. landscape—taking photos as he goes. At this stage, the emphasis is on his being *alone,* on the beach, in the car, in a diner and in a motel room. Each place is a space of transience and symbolises his separateness at all levels. Placing the Polaroids on the table in the diner, he says: "they never really show what you saw." This seeing/showing gap is explored throughout the film. In the motel —the Skyway motel which echoes the opening shot of the aeroplane in flight — Philip falls asleep foetally, a prelude to a whole series of references throughout the film to birth and parenting: the search for the mother and the father at a metaphorical level. When he wakes he smashes the television—it is showing a film about Abraham Lincoln—perhaps for it what represents as an image-reproducing machine; perhaps because the images of democracy conflict with his experience of his homeland, Germany; or perhaps it is simply a gesture of frustration and violence against the global dominance of American television imagery.

He sells his car as part of his preparation to leave America, takes a Polaroid of it but refuses to sell the camera. Putting on his sunglasses, he buys some German magazines and, in a sense, becomes a tourist as he boards the train at Shea Stadium—focus for a wide-angled shot of an archetypal American scene. At the office of his agent, we learn that Winter is a photojournalist with a story that he is unable to finish. Despite all the photographs and notes, he is incapable of combining image and narrative to create the story he was commissioned to produce about "the things you see . . . about signs and images." He has been on the road for four weeks to write about the American scene in popular culture. Driving across America, he says, the images you see make something happen. Wenders has argued that Germans turned to American culture so eagerly as a response to the gaps and absences in German postwar culture and an attempt to block out the memories of Nazism: "The need to forget twenty years created a hole, and people tried to cover this by assimilating American culture" (quoted in Sandford 1980: 104). The reason Winter took so many pictures is part of the story, he tells his agent, but he is unable to make the images *happen* and promises to complete the story in Germany. The agent tells him that he was not supposed to take pictures, but should have stuck to writing. This exchange between Winter and his agent announces the primary theme of the film—the failure of articulation between telling and showing, narration and image. The outsider in America can collect images but not give them meaning.

His attempt to return to Germany immediately is thwarted by a ground personnel strike and he is forced to delay his departure. At a hotel he plays with the child, Alice, in the revolving door, and helps her mother, Lisa, negotiate her travel back to Germany via Amsterdam. Lisa has just broken up with a man and, in response to Winter's: "I'm not very entertaining", says "you could be dumb for all I care." Both are anxious to leave the United States for different reasons, agree to travel together, but are not able to return directly. This *indirect* route back to Germany is significant for the development of the film's broader theme of the gap which opens up between signifier—urban, industrial Germany—and signified.

Before leaving, Winter visits the apartment of a woman friend, Angela, in New York. He confesses his disorientation and that he has lost his bearings and lost touch with the world, bruised by the sickening radio and inhuman TV of America. She responds that he has done that a long time ago and did not need to travel across America for that: "You lose touch when you lose your sense of identity . . . That's why you keep taking these photos . . . for further proof that it was you who saw something . . . that's why you came here to find someone to listen to you . . . listen to you and the stories you're really telling yourself." The woman and Winter speak simultaneously, not to, but at, each other.

Both Angela and Winter are operating with a positivist sense of identity which is fixed and accessible, and with a view of reality that is, in fact, arbitrary and contingent. Hence the profusion of photographs— "I went on as if I was possessed" (the photos are consuming him)— which never caught up with reality. With the traditional photograph there is a significant time-delay between the taking and developing of the image. The Polaroid camera speeds up the process and heightens the illusion of immediate correspondence between image and reality— "I could hardly wait to compare the picture with reality." What Winter discovers in Germany is that there is no anterior reality which images simply reproduce, but a whole world which has to be revisited and re-visioned before any *telling* can take place.

The woman sounds more like a mother than a lover when she says that she cannot help him but would like to comfort him: "I don't know how to live either. . . .no one showed me how." The only hint that she offers is that " in this city when you come to an intersection it's like coming to a clearing in the woods." The rest of the film is, for Winter, a series of intersections in various German cities; each one like a clearing in the woods which has to be decoded and made into an enabling narrative.

Winter learns that Alice and her mother have lived in four cities in two years. Lisa leaves Alice temporarily in Winter's charge but, ultimately, he has to take her on the flight to Amsterdam as her mother has returned to her lover, Hans. Initially, the prepubescent Alice and Winter explore the spaces between them, and he simply has functional responsibility for her evidenced by a series of static scenes in the hotel room, at the airport lounge, and on the plane. Different perspectives of the city are offered from the Empire State Building and from the plane; Winter takes a Polaroid photograph of the clouds, and Alice says: "that's a nice picture, so empty." From Amsterdam onwards, Alice becomes Winter's "maternal" guide (she has lived in the city) and the generational relationship is reversed as they travel through Germany filling up its "empty" images as seen by the child. In the Paul Joyce documentary mentioned earlier, Wenders says that the child's eye is the ideal point of view for a camera—blank, curious, no opinion; Alice lets the world come into her images, and Germany is seen as if for the first time because she is unable to remember anything. It is she who initiates conversation—"tell me something about yourself"—and wants to take photographs of him—"at least you'll know what you look like." The resulting photograph has Alice superimposed on his face, so their relationship goes beyond an instrumental responsibility and becomes a joint search for a lost Germany. Earlier, in Amsterdam, Winter has cut short the boat journey because he does not want to *see* anything.

The film explores the theme of the lost, or absent, mother and it is some time before Winter accepts his position as surrogate father. Mutually irritated by each other, they quarrel like peer nine year olds. When Alice asks him to tell her a story, he replies angrily that he does not know any. Later, when he offers to read her a story, assuming a fathering role, she is adamant that she does not want him to read to her as she can read by herself. This telling of stories and the difference between reading and being read to, widens into a broader metaphorical significance.

The only story that Winter tells Alice is of a little boy who gets lost:

Once there was a little boy who got lost. He went for a walk in the woods with his mother one lovely summer afternoon. . . . His mother suddenly felt tired and wanted a rest. All of a sudden the little boy heard a rustling in the bushes and he found a hedgehog. He ran after it until he came to a stream and in the stream he saw a fish. He ran along beside the stream till he saw a bridge. On the bridge was a horseman . . . .The boy went onto the bridge. Then he came to the highway. A street with lots of trucks. The boy sat at the roadside until a truck stopped and the driver asked if he would like a lift . . . He sat proudly next to the driver . . . And the boy rode as far as the sea. And at the sea he remembered his mother again.

The walk with the mother rehearses, what Kristeva calls, the semiotic *chora*, a moment prior to the entry into the Symbolic—the name of the father (Kristeva, 1984: 14). The bridge stages the encounter with differentiation and also, perhaps, with a classic figure of a preindustrial Germany—the fatherland. The highway repeats the phallic encounter in an urban, industrial setting: the place of the other, the locus of law and the Symbolic. These spaces of masculinity—this Germany of forest and autobahn, of trucks and radios (masculine spaces and artefacts)—have been, ultimately, destructive, and as the child is driven towards the sea (this echoes the opening sequences of the film) he reenters the semiotic *chora*, the mother's body, the undifferentiated spaces of the feminine. The story is Philip Winter's story as he searches Germany for Alice's mother, her mother's mother and, finally, the "maternal narrative" in himself. This is the story, his "scribbling", which he will complete in Munich. (The psychoanalytic aspects of Wenders's work will be explored more thoroughly in the chapter on *Paris, Texas*).

Throughout their journey across a range of German cities, Winter is always only the driver, and Alice always the guide, albeit one with an imperfect memory. This is partly because the Nazi experience has rendered Germany amnesiac—unmemorable—both incapable of memory and incapable of being remembered. Travelling across the cities is an act of anamnesis—the mobilising of memory. Only when he is able to recite a litany of German place names to Alice in alphabetical order is he able to begin a "story" of Germany; but at this stage he is dependent upon Alice to identify the significances and make the connections with her grandmother's house. Germany is, initially, a list of places, not a meaningful *place* for Winter with a set of cultural codes —the list is like the raw eggs mentioned by his woman friend in Manhattan: material for a narrative, not the narrative itself. Their search for Germany begins at the end of the alphabet, with Wuppertal— the first stage in the acquisition of a cultural, social and political literacy with which to *read* his country, find his home. At one point Alice says of his attempts to construct a narrative: "all you do is scribble in your book." The film is about bringing Germany into emotional legibility for the lost male of the immediate postwar generation.

Alice in the Cities is Wenders's first sustained attempt to come to terms with industrial, urban Germany in a format which is close to what Lyotard calls the *immemorial*—that which can be neither remembered (represented to consciousness) nor forgotten (consigned to oblivion). It is that which returns, uncannily (Readings, 1991: xxxii). The film is this *return*. The immemorial acts as a kind of *figure* for consciousness and its attempts at representing itself historically. The figure of Alice is not simply some Wordsworthian innocent through which Winter comes to "know himself" (as some critics like to maintain), but the superimposed photograph images a complex process in which the *singularity* of Germany is not lost in historical or positivist representation, with its past as something, that is, that merely happened. Similarly, in the photo booth they mimic/mirror each other, and, at one point, they do mock exercises in harmony. Their journey across the country goes beyond an individual search as it struggles to keep events from sinking into the oblivion of either representation (voice) or silence. The editing, with its series of distinct wipes, reinforces this process.

Alice's journey becomes Winter's when she realises that her grandmother has never lived in Wuppertal and it becomes his responsibility to chart their itinerary. At one point, he mentions that many of the older houses are going to be pulled down—another erasure of traces. Alice says that the empty spaces look like graves, house graves. In a sense their journey is "grave visiting"—the emptied and buried spaces of recent German history. He drives through the Ruhr district where he was brought up and went to school, returning to the "Alice phase" of his growth as he decides to leave her at the police station and continue his journey alone. He attends an open-air Chuck Berry concert and sits next to a girl who looks like an older version of Alice.

Alice slips away from the police when they leave her unobserved and rejoins Winter. Together they read her story in the newspaper; she is assuming the shape of a *public* narrative, a mediated existence. The whole film is about bringing Germany into *mediation*, finding images for re-presenting (rather than representing), making visible and accessible the empty signs/graves of meaning. Their interior, private narrative has to be expressed, made public.

Before Alice and Winter can have a directional and focused journey they have to complete one final rite of passage. On a beach, Alice wonders whether a woman sitting nearby thinks he is her father—the first specific reference she makes to this. Alice and the woman exchange banter which is based upon the woman assuming that he is her father, otherwise their relationship could take on a more sinister possibility. Winter and Alice, meanwhile, insult each other good-naturedly like squabbling children. The woman plays the surrogate mother for a while, and all three return to her hotel room for the night. Winter and the woman share a bed and, in a classic oedipal moment, Alice goes through a jealous phase. Waking early and seeing them in bed together, she looks at photographs of herself and Winter, feeling split by the new experience. She bids for his attention, sheds her androgynous child's clothing, and gets out her conventionally pretty dress—"growing up" to attract him away from the "other" woman (also her "mother" in a sense) by emphasising her own gender differentiation, previously muted in an extended pre-oedipal sequence entirely devoid of any traces of sexual precocity or cuteness. Waking him very early she asks him if he would not rather have slept alone. In this moment, she conflates all her various roles—the maternal feminine, daughter, lover. The unnamed woman rapidly evaporates, is "wiped" from the scene. What has happened is that Alice has resolved her own oedipal situation vicariously, through the role play of a substitute mother and father, thus repressing the possibility of actual incest.

The above analysis has concentrated upon the individual child (and the lost child in Philip Winter), but, metaphorically, the film extends this to the post-Nazi generation child —born in the 1960s—finding the missing generations. Like Carroll's Alice, the scale and perspective shifts as the child is alternately magnified and dwarfed by her experience in the cities, and her encounter with her figurative parents whom she also guides and "mothers". She remarks that he hasn't taken any pictures since Amsterdam; he has no need to because he sees/images Germany through her "telling eyes". Even his plan to visit his parents to ask for money is not followed through as the police catch up with them on the ferry and they learn about Alice's family in Munich. The journey would have been redundant anyway, as Alice, in her "parental" guise, has 100 dollars left over from America which is more than enough to pay both their fares.

The facts that, at the end, the police have traced Alice's mother and grandmother to Munich (with all its cultural significance as a symbolic centre of Nazism), and that Winter is able to accompany Alice by train to the city open up a new set of generational and gendered continuities and possibilities. Alice has provided the money for his ticket, again putting into uncertainty the precise dependency status of their relationship. Incidentally, we only see the adult, at last comfortable as a surrogate father, and child in transit; we can only assume they will arrive. Alice asks him what he will do in Munich and he replies that he will now be able to finish *this* story—image and narrative can begin to cohere. Her response—"your scribbling"—places it in perspective, a perspective which suggests that the "scribbling" is surplus to, and will never fit, the narrative which they, and we, have experienced. The last shot is of Winter and Alice looking out of the window as the camera takes up their point of view and pans across the landscape.

Missing Something With Every Movement

In *Wrong Movement* (1975) Wenders moves beyond the isolated pair travelling across, and drawing, an emotional map of a remembered Germany, and develops the film around an ensemble of characters moving (or, more precisely, *being moved* as they are so static and passive) from the north to the south of Germany. The ensemble consists of a writer, an acrobat/juggler, a musician, a poet, an actress and an industrialist. All, in some way or other, are producers and creators, people who work with the imagination, but each one is unproductive, awkward and solipsistic. They live in, or on, other people's sentences, their gestures are mechanical and borrowed, their performances are characterised by bad timing. Even the industrialist has to make several botched attempts before he finally kills himself.

The central figure, Wilhelm, is adapted from Goethe's *Wilhelm Meister's Apprenticeship*, and embarks upon a romantic journey in search of self. Detached and rigidly cast in, what one of the other characters calls, an objective pose, Wilhelm's quest is directionless and unfinished because what he observes he does not wish to see, and what he experiences involves other people in ways which do not square with his romantic preconceptions. Towards the end of the film, after the suicide of the industrialist, Wilhelm says: "The journey which I felt was a kind of work, I called off and we left in apathetic panic. We others stayed together but moved apart at the same time." The lost direction is always more than personal, as the landscape travelled through refuses to remain simply physical or pastoral. The urban and rural imagery articulates a series of questions about recent German history and politics which, while they are not answered, stubbornly insist on being asked. As with so many of Wenders's films in this period, evasion and indirectness mark out the emotional terrain—the spaces and timelapses take on cultural significance. The scale of the cinematography, the meticulous framing and the construction of the exterior shots all serve to emphasise the robotic and stylised, dysfunctional movement of the ensemble and minimises their scope for action and gesture. They are like the cast of an improvised play incapable of rehearsing or staging their performance because they are "muscle bound" by introspection, self-adjusted fantasy and the clichéd resources of obsolete paradigms.

Wilhelm—one of many unfulfilled writers in Wenders's films— smashes the window of his room as a dramatic attempt to break that which separates the self from its outside/not-self, cycles away from home, and rides alone on the ferry, a solitary figure in a rural landscape. The leaving of his mother and home town, the inability to communicate through his writing or with other people, and the search for belonging all help to constitute the initial trope of the isolated, suffering romantic artist. His shopkeeper mother places this in perspective by pointing out that he should not be intimidated by a positivist outlook in which people might say he is useless but that a doctor and a plumber are useful. This division in value, the contrast between the realm of action and the world of reflection, runs right through the film and remains unresolved. In fact, at the end, Wilhelm has retreated to an even more theatrical objective correlative of the romantic writer—the mountainous peaks of the Zugspitze: "I felt I had missed something and was missing something with every movement." Throughout the film, for all the endless talk, one feels a sense of things being forever deferred. Maybe the homogeneous "grand narrative" of Nazism has silenced all but a series of discrete and heterogeneous "little narratives".

The ensemble of characters form a set of eclipsed selves, confined in a contemporary moment which cannot yield meaningful connections, coherent narratives or personal relationships unless each figure is able to move beyond his or her surface experience, break the "freeze" of time and space, and find a voice which explicitly articulates the silences of memory, the gaps between them, and the lacunae in recent German history. As they walk and talk in relay formation along the mountain paths overlooking the Rhine, the rural idyll is punctured regularly by the sound of gunfire. At the end of this particular scene, we catch a brief shot of the hunter—the man of action—driving off on his motorcycle while the directionless and inactive figures move towards their temporary lodging. It is a brief reminder of an amnesiac Germany unable to confront its "monstrous" politics of violence. As the actress Therese, one of the ensemble, says: "Only when I keep remembering does a text sometimes makes sense," and she is speaking not only of a play text, but also of the film itself—a process of anamnesis—and of a divided Germany and its shared Nazi past.

There are several pairings within the ensemble which embody the wider issues I have referred to. Those that never pair are the unnamed industrialist and the effete, sentimental poet, Bernhard Landau (the very name suggesting a belonging to an obsolete age). Wilhelm and Therese occupy the centre of, what might be called, the personal dimension or "love interest" but their romance is derived from a set of fictional clichés and gets nowhere. Wilhelm and the old Nazi, Laertes, constitute the political realm. The division is shown to be specious, but the characters persist in treading its borderlines.

Wilhelm speaks to Laertes of his need to write politically and from a position of commitment, but realises that he feels estranged from politics: " I tried to write politically and realised words failed me. The words there meant nothing. I could not relate to them." Laertes responds that this might be a good reason to be politically active and drop writing altogether, but Wilhelm insists on the need to unite politics and poetry. This is true only at the level of rhetoric as it is obvious that, for Wilhelm, personal needs are all that is real for him. This is not only a post-Nazi reaction but also, perhaps, a response to the politics of 1968, a turning inwards and away from commitment. The books that Wilhelm takes with him on his journey are symptomatic: Eichendorff's *Diary of a Good-for-Nothing* and Flaubert's *L'Education Sentimentale*.

In a sense, whenever characters speak to each other in this film, they are effectively speaking to, and of, themselves—such is the distance between them and the level of self-entrapment. In the exchanges between Wilhelm and Laertes (the *Hamlet* references are obvious) there is another agenda being addressed: the isolated, post-war writer estranged from politics is trying to provoke answers from the representative of a previous, politically committed generation. The condition of the one's estrangement has its source in the other's refusal to remember, to bring his story into narrative. Laertes, the rundown street musician, hides behind his song and his harmonica, masking the fact that as an Olympic athlete in Berlin, in 1936, and as a concentration camp officer ("I saved some Jews if they were professionally qualified") he was the doyen of Nazi "manhood". His "muteness"—his guilt-induced nosebleeds and unwillingness to voice a collective past—is matched by his travelling companion, the actual mute, the child-woman Mignon, juggler, conjuror and acrobat. Her name has overtones of an earlier courtly role as sexual favourite, and Wilhelm reacts to her in an ambivalent way, alternately slapping and caressing her when he, mistakenly, embraces her naked body. Earlier in the railway carriage she had snuggled up to Wilhelm in child-like fashion and he had gone to the window to break the intimacy. In a bizarre fashion the street presence and (inept) performance of Laertes and Mignon is a shabby residue, pastiche almost, of the aestheticisation of politics which was a feature of Nazism as a public culture (the rail conductor's Nazi salute to Laertes is "remembered" by Wilhelm from old newsreels). Wilhelm's urge to kill Laertes, he acknowledges, is only a form of displacement: "My aimless rage was directed at the old man. I used his past as an excuse." All the figures in the text are using different pasts—cinematic, literary, political, cultural, economic—as an excuse for *inaction*, a generational paralysis: "expressing oneself with other people's sentences" as Therese says.

When Wilhelm says that it was as if he had to leave his mother behind in order to find her, we are reminded of the constant references throughout the 1970s films of the missing mothers and fathers of post-war Germany, and the search for surrogates. Mignon is apparently orphaned, with Laertes as a substitute grandfather; at the end, she goes off with Therese to form a new kind of bonding. The wife of the suicidal industrialist had recently hanged herself. They are of the "middle generation" and the man says that she often wished for a machine to stretch all the sinews of her body. The wife is the "missing mother" of the Nazi generation and her self-portrait is of a woman suspended in mid-air (as on a trapeze) with her clothes torn, her breasts and other parts of her body exposed. The rape imagery condenses a whole range of Nazi violations linked to the will to power.

In the industrialist's house, the ensemble form a kind of ersatz family with all generations and roles represented, including the hanged mother. The very theatricality of the setting—they are all initially framed in an arch like a cinematic still—heightens the artificiality and temporariness of their relationships, refugees from fear and intimacy, sitting round an archetypal family hearth with its log fire. The industrialist speaks of his loneliness—"I think it's more hidden and more painful than elsewhere"—and the soulless faces of Germany, and conceives of loneliness as a theatrical state which arises the moment you become aware of yourself as an actor. Each one in the ensemble is an actor—in the sense of rehearsing a series of borrowed identities—with the figure of Therese (dressed in the style of the Ingrid Bergman of the anti-fascist film *Casablanca*, frozen in a set of 1940s gestures) as an actual actress underscoring the theatricality of all her companions. She is the emblematic lover of screen romance and weaves her own web of romance around Wilhelm as writer. Like all the others she is time-warped, incapable of *immediacy*, moving through a set of overcoded and mediated poses framed by, and in, a wartime film; no images present themselves for a *post-war* understanding of Nazism.

At the outset, Wilhelm has realised that he does not like people, nor can he relate to them but feels intimidated and fearful. This fear is shared by all the characters in different ways. The industrialist articulates the situation most explicitly by saying that the German virtues like courage, fortitude and industry were all ways of overcoming fear, and that fear is considered vanity or shame, hence the need for a philosophy—Nazism—to mask it. As the man speaks he draws blood by pressing a pen into his hand, blood which Wilhelm uses on his notebook. This suggests that the one story he has to come to terms with before he can write anything else is of Germany's immediate blood-steeped past. He is incapable of such a narrative because, like all the others (Laertes scourges himself at night in a pastiche of a medieval monastic penance), he brings to this past the resources and models of representation which are forged in, and for, another era and are hopelessly inappropriate to the task. We are reminded of Adorno's words: there is no poetry after Auschwitz. Or it may be that an entirely new kind of poetry has to be imagined out of the dialectic of voice and silence.

Each character is "arrested" in the course of time, without shape or form, rather like the television in the room which flickers constantly without ever producing a coherent image, until they all move later to Therese's apartment where they watch a "classic" period romance in her shit-covered, graffiti-laden housing block. Again, the disjunction— the wrong movement—is clear. Even what they witness, they are unable to decode. The poet, Bernhard, dreams that their host, the industrialist, ran across a road and a cameraman pursued him. The host shouted, "Long live the exploited masses of the world," then he leapt and plunged down. The poet then had to look at the film as a witness. When they return to the lodge, they discover that the industrialist has

finally succeeded in killing himself. Only Wilhelm and Bernhard
witness this. In a sense, the film we are watching *is* the only witness as
it encodes the silences and evasions of post-war Germany, while the
characters are lost within the interstices of time and place and
fragments of memory and evidence. There are partial insights, like
Laertes's acknowledgment that "our defence of the natural led to
monstrous politics," but for the most part it is a pilgrimage without end
or purpose.

A Cowboy in Hamburg

The emotional illiteracy which is one of the themes of *The Scarlet
Letter*, *Alice in the Cities,* and *Wrong Movement* appears again in a
different form in *The American Friend* (1977) which was freely
adapted from Patricia Highsmith's novel *Ripley's Game* (1974).
Although the setting is predominantly European—mainly Hamburg—it
is a Europe where the American presence is strongly felt. The spaces in
the film are emphatically urban, with the amplified sounds and wide-
angled shots stressing movement and scale. Hamburg is a thriving
seaport, a point of intersection for trade and all kinds of other exchange.
The ships, the sound and movement of the trucks, the cranes, the
harbour, the cityscape, the subways, the discords of screeching seagulls
and atonal piano sounds, the heights, distances, shapes and colour all
suggest motion and restlessness—a scale of activity beyond the human.
In this context the domestic and the settled, parental and marital
relationships seem marginal to the sounds of the city. As with *Alice in
the Cities*, this is a film concerned with images at a number of different
levels. At the centre of the film is a double preoccupation with value
and truth. Into the city of commodity exchange, a painting by a
supposedly dead artist, Derwatt, is introduced and offered for auction.
The painting is a fake but it still reaches a high price. Its value depends
upon its purchaser not knowing, not seeing. Not seeing is, in fact,
believing. This introduces the central motif: the confusion of truth and
falsehood brought into focus by a range of optical instruments which
produce different visual illusions.
The figure of Tom Ripley is the key dissembler, the go-between for
the fake-art trade and the man who sets in train the principal events of
the narrative by setting up the Hamburg frame-maker, Jonathan
Zimmermann. Ripley—the (highly equivocal) American friend—
summarises in his person many of the deceptions and contradictions
throughout the film. By using Dennis Hopper, the director of *Easy*

Rider, to play the part of Ripley, and two other American film directors, Sam Fuller and Nicholas Ray, as actors, Wenders is doing more than simply producing a *hommage* film, or displaying skills in cultural quotation. He is using the full resources of cinematic technique to raise questions about cultural truth, fictionality and the limitations of the representational as the fundamental premise of a realist aesthetic. At the same time he produces a film with elements which place it generically in the mainstream of American popular culture—the *film noir*.

While Ripley simply acts as broker (for the paintings, for setting up Jonathan as a "hit man"), he wears a cowboy hat combined with worker"s overalls, signifying a melange of gendered genre belonging— "what's wrong with wearing a cowboy hat in Hamburg," he asks Nicholas Ray. This (apparent) incongruity is at the heart of the film and acts as a signifier of the popular cultural presence of America in Germany, apart from any geopolitical significance brought about by the Cold War. Ripley discards the hat when he role-switches later in the film and becomes a *noir* killer to assist Jonathan. Ripley, rootless, displaced, unattached and emotionally illiterate, symbolises the homo-erotic world of masculinised genre fictions, and seeks to befriend Jonathan in what starts out as a kind of game. It is actually much less of a game in the film than it is in the novel where Ripley is married and remains relatively detached from Jonathan. In the film, there is a sense in which, apart from having been piqued by a remark of Jonathan's ("I have heard of you") and the fact he refused to shake hands with him, that Ripley is trying to seduce Jonathan from the settled world of family, home and work to share his alienation and emotional hollowness. Jonathan seems to occupy a moral ground which Ripley seeks to challenge, perhaps in order to show its instability and lack of depth, or maybe simply out of envy. It may not be too fanciful to see it in the Jamesian terms of European maturity and American callowness. It is ironic that Ripley is so successful in luring Jonathan into the amoral that he tells Minot of Ripley's involvement in the mafioso murder when they had agreed to keep it a secret.

Jonathan Zimmermann (the confined and circumscribed "room man") is a traditional craftsman, with a wife and young son, suggesting roots and affiliations which predate late capitalist values and, perhaps, Nazi Germany also. Ripley lures him out of his room metaphorically, and out of his frame (he is a picture frame maker and restorer)—the limits and confines of his ordered, petit-bourgeois shopkeeper life. Belonging nowhere, a creature of the streets and the city, Ripley learns that Jonathan has a blood disease and, by simulating a letter from a friend who hints that his illness may be worse than he thinks, suggests to a criminal acquaintance (Raoul Minot) that Jonathan might be tempted into acting as a hit man for the right price if he thinks he is dying. By introducing doubt and uncertainty into his world, Ripley provokes Jonathan into a life of dissimulation, risk, adventure and violence which he justifies to himself on the grounds that the money he will receive for the murders will go to his family after his death.

Jonathan, who inhabits a milieu characterised by bourgeois values of truth, authenticity, family values, hard work and deferred gratification—he restores original paintings and frames works of aesthetic value —is plunged into a world of lies and violence. The man, wedded in all kinds of ways to the literal and the real, embarks upon a life in which he is forced to improvise, to make up his own narrative, to dwell in the arbitrary and the contingent. His medical reports are faked by contacts of Minot, but he can never be certain who holds the truth—his bourgeois family doctor or the specialists in Paris and Munich—or, indeed, if such a thing as truth exists at all. He begins to live as if he *is* dying, which raises questions as to whether his morality was conditional on the assumption of a "normal" life. The reactive man, dependent upon the wishes and values of others, leaves his "secondary" life to become primary and proactive, the author/auteur of his own narrative.

What Ripley is doing is directing Jonathan in a *film noir* (based, according to Kolker and Beicken, on Ray's 1950s thriller *Bigger Than Life*) in which there is a strong element of play, with Jonathan forced to become an "actor" committed to an exciting world of risk and danger. The moment when, back in his shop, he angrily breaks a frame marks his shift from one mode of existence to another. Throughout the film, Wenders uses another visual signifier of the shifting worlds. In all the domestic and work scenes, Jonathan wears a striped football scarf and a woollen cap, signs of his parenting and marital role. In the all-male gangster world of violence the scarf and the cap are discarded as markers of the banal and the settled. Only in the final sequences of the film when the domestic and the public world of violence converge does he resume the "uniform" of fatherhood, but by this time it is too late to save himself. The last scene features an excluded Ripley, and Jonathan's wife, Marianne, on the bleached white sands of the seashore —the place of the "remembered mother". The "paternal" mafiosi of the *noir* scenes, the homo-social world of Ripley, and the dangers of the masculinised narrative are all consumed and displaced as gendered and generational illusions/fictions which have exhausted their significance as resources of cultural meaning.

The blood which marks the masculine romance of the thriller and the western genre runs like a motif throughout the film, beginning with the credits, focusing on the scarlet furnishings of Ripley's room, and settling on Jonathan's leukaemia, and raises obvious questions about male anxiety and female "nature" (Jonathan only touches his wife, Marianne, when she is asleep—there are virtually no other women in the film). As I said earlier, Ripley's status as friend is always equivocal; he seems to need a surrogate, a literal "partner in crime", someone who will *act for him*, as he draws the line at murder until he decides to aid Jonathan in the second killing. But throughout the film what is really interrogated is the "American" of the title. Ripley needs a mirror of himself; he needs to strip and empty Jonathan of his relationships, bind him to himself in his nomadic and unstable state, so that he can justify himself to himself in the end. Why otherwise does he lie back on the pool table (stock image from the American male film) and shower Polaroid images of himself on top of himself? He also constructs a kind of daily record of himself on a tape recorder, although the little we hear seems to be a set of clichés. In a bizarre sense he is only really able to reproduce himself by giving birth to or creating Jonathan—hence his role has to be played by a film director, a maker of fictions/fantasies. At the same time, Jonathan can only make meaning out of his life by becoming an actor inserted in a series of *film noir* set-pieces. In the words of the novel, "He was imagining being another person" (Highsmith, 1974: 53), licensed to kill, so to speak, by his apparently fatal illness. Morality works so long as we are not presented with the opportunity of being another person at any other level than that of fantasy—one of the functions of cultural fictions. At another point in the novel, Jonathan says, "he could pretend to be acting, in someone else's clothes, pretend the gun was a blank gun in a play" (Highsmith, 1974: 71).

Similarly, American power depends upon a complicit and passive, divided Germany. Later in the film, Ripley sings a line from the old Woody Guthrie song "Pity the Poor Immigrant"—the pity is self-pity, the migrant is himself condemned to a life of wandering, which is why he wants subconsciously to break Jonathan from the frame of his settled life. Apart from this local level of interpretation, what forces are at work to persuade a German to kill a Jew from northwest New Jersey (this is not in the book), and what was it that made Wenders change the domestic location of the book from Fontainebleau to Hamburg? In fact, why is it that both murder victims in the film (but not in the book) are American? The political is not confronted directly but American power is analysed through the seductive ambivalences of its popular cultural forms, in particular those which are articulated around fantasies of masculinity. To see this as simply a manifestation of Wenders' "love affair" with American movies is to misunderstand profoundly the nature of his deep critical engagement with American cultural hegemony and postwar German political identities.

Chapter 2

Living in the Borderlands: Masculinity in Crisis

In Vic Seidler's book *Unreasonable Men* he shows how the identities of men have been shaped by particular histories, cultures and traditions (Seidler, 1994). Reason and rationality in western society have come to be regarded as the natural basis of the dominant forms of heterosexual masculinity. Masculinity, reason, progress and logic were identified with the control and domination of nature, including a particular version of human nature.

In recent years, it has been commonplace to see masculinity as restless and, in what Susan Faludi has called the "backlash", women are being blamed for a crisis in gender values which has seemed to produce an increase in male violence and associated forms of pathological behaviour towards women. So-called coherent identities which stemmed from a specific model of masculinity are no longer available. Above all, the traditional boundary between reason and emotion has been transgressed. The white, middle class "feeling man" came and went, and, it is argued, we seem to have arrived at a position in which men are becoming marginalised.

In tracing the development of certain themes in Wenders's films, I am examining the devaluation of nature, disdain for the body, and masculinity as a constant source of anxiety. Imagination, dreams and fantasies have been conventionally scorned as forms of "unreason", and Wenders's territory is the rediscovering of cultural spaces for these through the medium of film in the context of the poverty in the language of relationships—men to men, as well as men to women. Questions of power, morality and gendered behaviour are located in the literal and metaphorical borders of post-war, divided Europe, particularly West Germany. In Wenders, fascism is not explored as an aberration that marks a breakdown of reason, but as a continuing and informing presence which has been masked by German culture. He also sees particular forms of gendered behaviour as being articulated with authoritarian power systems.

A lack of an interior life is seen to characterise dominant forms of masculinity based upon a "denial" culture which leaves little space for desire, and in which emotions are seen as being in need of redemption. Any unmediated, originating feelings are suspect and we learn to silence them. Mediation takes many forms, including structure, screen, mask, pose, gesture and trained/inherited body language. In this way, particular forms of masculine experience become legitimated. Masculinity requires vigilance, especially against eruptions and excesses of nature. The body is discounted as a source of identity, and feelings are "othered". Policing the body is part of the way in which autonomy becomes identified as masculine.

As I have said, relationships and gendering take place within particular cultural and historical settings. For Wenders it is the generation growing up in post-1945 Germany with a fear of intimacy and of sharing themselves, yet often characterised by emotional dependency disguised as a projection away from the self of desire and affectivity. In *Kings of the Road* (1976), the figure of Bruno seems to take pride in not having any emotional needs—he is self-contained and mobile. Not only is he on the road, but like many of Wenders's men, he is *on the run*.

Masculinity in its dominant forms seeks to establish identities in terms of fixities, whereas the films make it possible to think of the contingent character of identities. Wenders returns values and meanings to their cultural contexts, and concentrates upon isolating and redefining the parameters of masculinity, in the process recognising complex and differentiated gendered behaviour. He works on the reason/nature border as well as on the homo-erotic border with a visual economy which stresses affective inarticulacy through spatial relationships, fragmentation and displacement, framing and positioning. In Durkheim's words, what we see is that " the man that we try to be is the man of our times and our milieu" (quoted in Seidler, 1994: 128) set in a problematic and crisis-engendered context. The issue of sustained or sustaining relationships is implicit throughout the films of the 1970s and early 1980s, and becomes more explicit with the later films.

Women are frequently seen as devalued and supplementary "others", and their difference presents itself to the paranoid male as concealing secrets/knowledge/power which have to be violated in order to be revealed. The inner cannot be tolerated; it has to be yielded and controlled, made public—hence rape and other forms of violence. Even differentiated responses can provoke violence, especially signs of vulnerability.

Wenders's films are working at points of crisis and exhaustion in terms of affective illiteracy and a transitional vocabulary of masculinity. For example, in *Until the End of the World* (1991) we see the exhaustion of a scientific paradigm which has brought the world close to apocalypse, and a rational/technological masculinity associated with the "death drive" and the paternal agency. In a different light, in *Faraway, So Close!* (1993) dominant forms of masculinity are articulated closely with a capitalist moral culture and its emotional economy, subjected to parody, with space being made for, what might be called, an ethical masculinity linked to the possibility of differently gendered behaviour and models of relationship.

In some ways all of Wenders's films are concerned with frontiers and borders, but a number are specifically related to actual borders/frontiers which take on a symptomatic role at the level of the political, cultural, sexual and historical. Though always metaphorical, the borderline is never only metaphorical, as the films work very precisely with specific cultural and historical contexts—the postwar rootlessness of West Germany, the new globalisation, and post-Cold War Europe. These contexts are also spaces for the analysis of gendered behaviour, places where the gap or hole at the border of subjectivity (what Kristeva calls the *abject*) threaten to engulf the individual when its identity is threatened. The abject is "the place where meaning collapses" and which disturbs identity, system and order. It can never be fully set apart from the subject or society, so we almost obsessively seek to remove its traces. In *The Goalkeeper's Fear of the Penalty* (1972) we see a figure detached and drifting for whom all meaning has collapsed, whereas in *Kings of the Road* we witness endless strategies deployed to prevent meaning from collapsing.

In the latter film Bruno copes with one form of abjection when he expels his bodily waste in the sand so that he might continue to live, shortly after taking on a travelling companion, Robert. At the end, however, Robert calls him a corpse when he accuses him of lacking desire and the wish to change. According to Kristeva, the corpse is the ultimate in abjection as it is a body which can no longer expel its waste—it is a border that has encroached upon everything: the "I" is expelled.

Characters live in the borderlands, which means that their masculine subjectivity is never really clear of that which separates it from all which menaces its existence. The films explore the ways in which this menace is made sense of, repressed or projected, although it is more problematic than it sounds because the abject not only repels, it also fascinates. As the abject is identified with the feminine and the maternal, the absence and presence of women in the films are a source of potential disturbance for the "borderline" male.

The Goalkeeper begins and ends in a classic masculine location—a football stadium—and focuses upon competition, achievement, goals and performance, with a small number of specialist professionals in the public realm subject to the look/scrutiny of a larger number of critical males expecting competence, skill and, above all, success. The professionals are absorbed in and by their work, defined by the striving which gives them their meaning. The goalkeeper is in a double-edged situation: by preventing the other team from scoring he secures victory for his own team, but the converse is also true. His role is that of border watcher, the last line of defence. In this particular context, the goalkeeper Josef Bloch's uncertainty, his conceding of an easy goal and his sending-off for protesting to the referee (the paternal symbolic, in Kristeva's terms) all weaken his team. As they are playing away, their vulnerability is increased. The film begins, therefore, in a context of weakness, failure and anxiety as these are all articulated within a specific cultural form of masculinity: the performative spectacle.

The "anxious" aspects of the look of the male are here embodied; in *Kings of the Road* the look is allayed by drawing upon the structures of fetishistic looking and by displacing it from the male body as such and locating it more generally in the overall components of highly ritualised scenes, especially of the road and of the landscape. In *Goalkeeper* the look is attached more to the male body which is why he is so restless. He is also, of course, being sought for murder and, towards the end, an identikit photograph of him appears in the paper, thus compounding the look.

Josef Bloch appears directionless and unintegrated. His defence against excessive anxiety is depleted and he regresses to the stage of the infant ego: "Trauma implies that the baby has experienced a break in life's continuity, so that primitive defences now become organized to defend against a repetition of 'unthinkable anxiety' or a return of the acute confusional state that belongs to disintegration of the nascent ego structure" (Winnicott, 1988: 114). Unthinkable anxiety and an acute confusional state characterise Josef's actions and behaviour for much of the film. In Melanie Klein's terms anxiety arises from the operation of the death instinct within the organism, and is felt as a fear of annihilation and takes the form of paranoia. Josef's lack of cohesion (his friend Hertha is exasperated by his untidiness), his detachment and his withdrawal from all but functional language and communication have been interpreted as existential alienation and comparisons made with Camus' *L'Etranger*. It is also possible, however, to view it from a psychoanalytical position, seeing his condition as a breakdown in differentiation and individuation from the mother—a failure in relationship with external objects. The seemingly unmotivated murder of Gloria, a cinema cashier and one-night stand, the flight from the city into the rural borderlands of Austria and his dissociated absence/presence throughout the main part of the film all suggest an incompleteness and displacement which are consistent with "a continuing existence of intense anxiety [which] will disrupt symbol formation allowing for the continuation of splitting and projection and psychotic or autistic elements in individuals" (Rutherford, 1992: 52).

Thus, instead of objects and events in the world being invested with displaced meanings, objects and events are experienced with detachment (he makes no attempt to stop the ball going in the net) and emptied of meaning, and the individual (Josef) is carrying an unresolved splitting and projection process which produces aggression and paranoia (e.g. on the football pitch, at the inn, towards the telephonist). No mourning is felt for the death of the woman—strangled as she lay on her bed with her legs in a position ambiguously suggesting birth and/or sexual intercourse (abjection, Kristeva says, is, above all, ambiguity). It is this position which seems to provoke a "memory" which, in turn, gives way to sadistic violence. The body must bear no trace of its debt to nature: it must be clean and proper in order to be fully symbolic. Gloria's position is seen as transgressive— her body's debt to nature revealed. Josef seeks to remove all traces of himself from the objects in the room, overlooking an American coin which has slipped out of his sight and which will reappear in a newspaper report of the murder.

Josef takes a long bus journey by night until he arrives at the frontier of Austria and Hungary—a Cold War borderline. Here he tries to re-establish a relationship (in a passive way) with a former girlfriend, Hertha Gabler. The relationship is frustrated by the presence of a child and an absent, rarely glimpsed but potential husband, the estate owner's son. As I have said, Josef's failure as a goalkeeper indicates an incompleteness in his individuation, and his *indifference* suggests a desire to return to an undifferentiated relationship with the mother-surrogate, Hertha. She is the natural, mother-like figure in the daytime (a "good" object), but in the evening becomes the made-up and sexualised woman for the men in the bar which she runs: she is another borderline figure. In their only nocturnal encounter, her false eyelashes and hairpiece are emphasised, and Josef indirectly calls her a "painted cow" (the abject/whore/"bad" object): the sexually voracious woman who threatens the male; she is Paglia's "chthonic" woman (Paglia, 1995).

Josef's desire for *incorporation*, to be taken into the body of the woman and to cease to be the *other*, accounts for his "arrested" positionings—his loss and displacement in the far from idyllic rural border. At the castle he learns the story of a man who was found hanging because the darkness of the spruce forests had made him lose his wits; this suggests that he may have found the chaos of nature, its chthonic qualities, overwhelming. The man is an analogue of Josef. Cuts and camera movements isolate, disconnect him and render him inconsequential with a hollow, incoherent subjectivity.

This "absence" is supplemented narratively by the recurring motif of the death of a deaf-mute schoolboy drowned in the brook; his disappearance had been reported on daily in the local press, alongside the reports of Gloria's murder and the search for her killer. In a sense, the deaf-mute child is a symbolic displacement of Josef who reads press accounts of the murder with indifference, even commenting on an identikit picture as if he were a third person. Anxiety generates a death-wish: was he killing Gloria, or a fantasy of an undifferentiated self within Gloria? Several women of Gloria's age move through the narrative, tangentially in touch with Josef.

Klein places the figure of the mother at the centre of subject formation and sees symbol forming as a defence mechanism against anxiety (Rutherford, 1992: 95). Josef's relationship with the external world breaks down in the football stadium where he becomes preoccupied and immobilised. Gloria is the second pick-up in a brief space of time. She tells him of the dream in which she is wearing a dress made of bank notes which is crackling because it's on fire. The fire extinguisher becomes a flame thrower (later in the film Josef tells two women at a bus stop of his dream in which he acts with fire extinguishers). In Freud, fire is associated with male sexuality, a symbol of the libido. Gloria has dreamed her own death.

In a sense, Josef has overcome the conflict with the mother's body in fantasy, but instead of searching for new conflict-free relationships with substitute-objects, he repeats the fantasy with Hertha (significantly, Hertha has no room for him at her inn, literally and metaphorically). He is not able to exceed the transformational position of the mother.

The Goalkeeper is an instance of masculinity in a particular class, professional and period context confronted by the *presence* of the female. *Kings of the Road*, in a different context and in a different set of relationships, is characterised by the absence or passivity of women.

This film is Wenders's most explicit road movie—a film about space and movement, motion and emotion. It was shot in eleven weeks from July to October 1975 between Lüneberg and Hof along the East German border. It is literally, as well as metaphorically, set on the frontier, in a geopolitical area symptomatic of the wider Cold War—a site of tension and instability, another cultural form of masculinity — public, conflicted, and binarised. It is a precise cultural context in which a range of specifically masculine gendered problems are exposed, focusing on male/male relationships. These are very much what might be called the presences of the narrative—sometimes to excess—but the mother/father absences are also a crucial intertext.

The settings are rural small town with landscapes whose spaces are emphasised and contrasts sharpened by the use of black and white film throughout. There are two principal figures. Bruno, a cinema repair technician, lives and works from a mobile transporter, on the road. The truck is home, a living museum of old cinema technology, and his moving space-time vehicle. It contains him and he is safe, master, within its confines. It is the site of his cultural authority and

his masculine potency is preserved through his compulsion to move in adventure, in life on the road. . . .The fantasies of his omnipotence ensure that he never stops long enough to be consumed by his predicaments. To be still and passive is to herald the image of a small boy who still belongs to his mother and cries out for protection. Mastery is achieved by clinging to continuity and to linear time. (Rutherford, 1992: 129)

In *Goalkeeper*, Josef adjusts a clock and changes a calendar to the correct date; the German title of *Kings of the Road* is *In the Course of Time*. Bruno avoids those spaces which threaten fusion and the loss of self. This fear of fusion, in Rutherford's terms, is translated into a fear of association. He must remain solitary and mobile, in his rig, his gaff (as the final song says).

Each stop, every moment of stillness and passivity, is a potential trauma, except when it involves Bruno working on cinema equipment. With this he is impersonal, strong and effective—absorbed and defined, symbiotic, his meanings expressed in the skills he deploys, with only a thin relationship to his inner self. He wears work overalls throughout. He is independent and self-sufficient, but vulnerable because of a nostalgia for a threatened form of cinema and a specific technology. In terms of my gendered analysis, he is the master of image, focus and composition (Paglia's Apollonian man of culture and art) as, by working on projection, he controls the "look" and displaces it from the male body and its anxieties, ensuring the mediated and the indirect. This is made explicit at one point where he edits part of a trailer for a soft pornography film into a continuous loop, so that it will run nonstop in the projector: "Brutality, Action, Sex! Ninety minutes of film that television cannot show . . . ," the soundtrack says repeatedly. Classic masculinist "look" images of rape, a house collapsing in flames, and a woman's breasts heaving are shown constantly. He watches this, dispassionately, with the cinema cashier, Pauline, who sits not next to him but behind him and tells him of a woman who had vaginal cramp in the cinema and as the couple could not withdraw from intercourse, they had to be taken to hospital. This encodes yet another standard male anxiety—the *vagina dentata*—and links with comments I shall make later about Bruno and his fear of intercourse. The fact that he is continuously involved with projection almost needs no gloss, as it suggests an uncompleted maturation and separation from the mother.

As I have said each stop on the road is potentially traumatic, and the first such incident is marked by the intrusion of, and possible fusion with, Robert Lander, who drives his VW into the river in a half-hearted suicide attempt. Bruno offers him assistance, dry clothes and a lift to the next town. They remain together for the duration of the film, but the time span is never specified—it is an extended spatial moment. Robert is a psycholinguist who works on children's initial acquisition of writing and reading skills. Their meeting, and his occupation indicate an exploration of uncompleted masculinity, of a traumatised subjectivity.

The working out of the film's themes takes place around five principal episodes: the rear-screen pantomime in a cinema for children; an encounter with a man of their age—thirty something—whose wife has committed suicide; a visit by Robert to his father, coinciding with Bruno's meeting with Pauline at the fairground and cinema; a journey back to their respective childhood spaces; and a final encounter between the two of them in a disused American frontier post.

The rear-screen pantomime segment indicates how Wenders articulates particular forms of masculinity through a visual language of proximity, synchronisation and distance, a spatial vocabulary which expresses a certain affective illiteracy (or fear of affectivity) and anxiety about intimacy, fusion and incorporation (the taking in of the body). As Wilhelm Reich realised, "being estranged from our bodies is part of a larger displacement of our emotional selves that we have also learned to treat as part of a separated nature" (quoted in Seidler, 1994: 133). Early on, Robert asks Bruno "where's your home, your base?" He replies, "the van is registered in Munich. I bought it there."

Robert has left his wife (in Genoa) but remains dependent upon her, evidenced by the frequent attempts at phoning her, although he has torn up the photograph of their house (with its links to the body, her body). Both men fear each other's closeness, suggesting anxiety about some primal loss and separation, a failure in maturation and individuation — in effective symbolisation. The encounter with the man whose wife committed suicide is a turning point which partially releases them from their stasis and deadlock.

The man's wife had suddenly had enough of domesticity and drove straight into a tree (returning to the chthonic), killing herself. The moment of telling is marked by numerous silences and pauses, and cuts to each man's face, which indicate the difficulty of men entering into affective language. Robert tentatively offers help; at first, the man is threatening and paranoid. He is wearing his wife's bloodstained coat, thus still dependent on her and, perhaps, identifying with the anxiety and despair which produced her death instinct (it may also signify a sublimated wish to kill her); the blood is a marker of the miasmic space of nature, of the female body, of the chthonic. In a sense, the episode recoups a primal scene: the man cannot face seeing the car (womb) being removed, and wants to stay in the van. Robert, sitting closely framed with the man, says they have to move on, anxious to shed the emotional proximity. Bruno says they don't have to move on, but unable to take the physical and emotional confinement he wanders off, visits the car wreck—metonym of the female body—and finds a distant, disused observation tower as a way of restoring the sovereignty of the look, displacing it from the male body, and separating himself from the personal and the affective. Robert and the man remain framed in an enclosed one-shot—the man crouches almost as if to touch him, but his head is averted.

This episode comes close to, what in psychoanalysis is called, the depressive position (cf the man's initial body posture, foetally hunched over a derelict quarry shaft) and the fear of object loss: "[it is] a fundamental moment in the structuring of the human psyche, when splitting and projection are overcome and a new relation to reality is introduced" (Rutherford, 1992: 124). The last shot of the man is without his wife's coat, suggesting a birth image and a transition into the realm of the Symbolic. The depressive position is "the inception of subjective historicity"—the entry into thought and language. Metaphorically, the woman/mother has brought about an effective moment of growth and development—of symbolisation—for all three men: a maturational process in which excessive anxiety is defended against. They are, so to speak, "on the road" again, although there is no simple form of redemption effected. Relationships between the two principals remain conflicted and, ultimately, unresolved: trapped in the abstract, impersonal discourses of masculinity.

Nevertheless, Robert is released temporarily from deadlock and decides to visit his father in Ostheim, a journey he makes alone after negotiating several obstacles and barriers. The journey to the father, after the lapse of a decade, has political and psychoanalytical implications. His father is a newspaper editor and printer—the realm of thought and language, the paternal signifier and the mediated—with generational roots in the Nazi period. When they meet—significantly in the public sphere of work as if it embodies him entirely—the father puts his hands on his arms but Robert holds up an admonishing finger. "Listen to me", he says and, disengaging from his grasp, asks "still doing everything alone?"—in the realm of rational masculinity, that is. "All these ten years away whenever I think of something or talk about something . . . the first thing I do is imagine it in print" (another reminder of the mediated discourse of rationality, a gendered mode of obliqueness). Robert silences his father frequently, but remains silent for three hours himself: "you just babble on. Mother couldn't get a word in either." Father tears paper from the typewriter as a sign of recognition, of surrender. The scene is a working through of the oedipal situation, restoring the (dead) mother if only in the mediated form of a lead article written and printed by Robert while the father sleeps. The only way he can approach his father is via his medium—newsprint: "How to Be Able to Respect a Woman" (at least, he says, piously, I separated from my wife, although it is not as sacrificing as he suggests; Bruno asks if there shouldn't be a question mark). The encounter rehearses the good father/bad father scenario of the psychoanalytical paternal narrative, the return of the maternal supplement with its potential collapse of boundaries—the abject on the border. However, the parting embrace between son and father suggests the restoration of the good father enabling contact with those "helpful objects" symbolised in, what is known as, "the third term", a transitional space between inner and outer. The father tells him that his own mother had died in childbirth, indicating a legacy in a particular cultural form of masculinity—a fear of the maternal, of loss and separation never fully externalised in symbolic form. I have stressed the father/son conflict but the whole exchange also has, as I have hinted earlier, a wider psycho-political dimension.

Intercut with this episode, simultaneously, is Bruno's meeting with a woman, Pauline, at a fairground. Carrying a Hitler icon (a piece of fairground junk) she gives Bruno money, mistakenly, for a ride on the dodgems—for an extended moment she moves freely and unimpeded, alone in the arena, until she is stopped by the attendant who steers her to the margins, her brief interlude in space eclipsed. Bruno visits the cinema, where she works as a cashier, flirts with her, complains about the film's quality and takes over the projection booth, adjusting the focus, splicing film and so on, as if he could not stand too much leisure and inactivity—pleasure and spontaneity being the realm of the repressed mother. Pauline is a single parent: "I live alone with my daughter and I always will." They spend the night together, but passively and languidly, in the same space but separate, uninvolved. Pauline's look is unvaried—passive, repressed, sad, resigned, enclosed and framed alone. Her situation embodies another specific cultural/political moment—missing fathers (Bruno's died in the war) and evasive masculine responsibility, in flight from the affective realm, cocooned in the narcissistic (her cousin is shown in the projection booth masturbating to the soft porn movie which he has back-projected onto a wall).

The intercutting is not simply technical, because Pauline is linked symptomatically with Robert's dead mother—the woman as passive supplement. Bruno, like Robert's father, is master of, and at home with, the machine. One edit shows Bruno and Robert working, synchronically but at a distance, on technical apparatus —print/film — absorbed, controlling and detached in symbiotic male action, against stillness and passivity, *on behalf of women* but protecting themselves. Bruno takes a tear from Pauline's cheek and brushes it against his own, but it is a distantiating move, an appropriation, a transference of ownership, against the fear of incorporation and fusion (a hug, for example). When the possibility of fusion occurs, there immediately follow images of spaciousness, long shots, slow takes on the road, visual gaps and silences—movement *away from*, not towards.

The penultimate stage sees both men closer than ever, returning to a scene of Robert's childhood, borrowing an old motorcycle combination and, nostalgically, driving through scenes of childhood, constantly shifting positions from bike to sidecar—almost as if, after the enclosed quasi-domestic spaces, they need to put speed and distance between them. It is also the high point of their fusion—buddies on the road, boyish release and freedom: a journeying back in time. This is followed, however, by a return to a house that Bruno knew as a child on an island in the Rhine. The house was hidden in summer; it is another primal scene, linked to the mother. Bruno tells Robert they cannot sleep in the house, which becomes identified with the body of the mother (Robert never enters it, although he approaches the threshold). Inside the house, Bruno smashes a window, perhaps to open access to the external—an attempt at symbolisation.

Bruno finds a tin, concealed years before, with a comic strip book inside it. While Robert sleeps in the grounds, Bruno is awake all night in some kind of vigil—shortly before dawn (a moment associated with death imagery) he is seen weeping briefly at a "primeval" loss and separation, but he soon controls himself. Almost all of this sequence is shot at night or in half-light, suggesting liminality, a border moment. Unusually, when they leave, Bruno asks Robert to drive the combination. Their movements have become more synchronised, even regressive (Bruno skips, childlike, when they enter the garage housing the combination). Their earlier walking/running away from the cinema is in synch and Chaplinesque. In the cab they sing together "Just like Eddie."

But the mood is not allowed to consolidate, as Bruno becomes more introspective. His words, "I suddenly see myself as someone who has lived through a time and that time is my history" extend into a specific cultural context—the 1960s male. They arrive at the borderland and realise they can't go on, literally and metaphorically. The final scene in the deserted, American border hut breaks down their synchronisation, their fusion and association. The concluding shots set up space between them, each is framed in isolation and from a distance, in a divided-up composition, with the separated mattresses and windows contributing to a visual register of evasion, fear and separation.

Although they are on the border, they both are in retreat and are unable to achieve that "third space between inner and outer, the condition of a border: a border that mediates the spatial and atemporal sphere of instinctual affects and the historical and contingent relations of cultural life" (Rutherford, 1992: 104). The film has traced this border throughout, but neither character can fully come to terms with the mother's absence and respond to the demand for a representation of an objectively perceived reality. This border is closer to the one described earlier —the place of the abject where meaning collapses, that gap or hole at the border of subjectivity.

The border "implies the protection of one's self from crossing over it or from being crossed over and into" (Rutherford, 1992: 105). On this literal border, each self becomes a moving frontier and no longer distinguishes between space and time, inner and outer, subject and object. Both men suffer from separation anxiety which they disguise by antagonism, even fighting at one point because their comments cut too close for comfort. Robert will return to his wife because he is afraid "she may do something," although he says, "I am no longer myself when I am with her" and because, as Bruno suggests, he is afraid for himself. He accuses Bruno of having no desire, that he is like a corpse in a bunker - with the "I" expelled. Bruno replies that he has desire for a woman, any woman: "all women arouse my desire, so I don't get involved any more." The defensiveness of this position, and the absence of any reference to relationships, is exposed when he says: "when you fuck you're inside a woman, but have you ever felt close to her? . . . I always felt lonely inside a woman . . . lonely to the core."

Apart from the obvious castration anxiety, this indicates an incomplete withdrawal of the infant ego from the maternal, and links with his response to Robert when he is describing a child who used to see letters as figures in a narrative. The child says the letter E was "stupid and lazy, a crook, living in the underworld, dirty and evil"; Bruno cuts across this by humming "mean as she could be," tying the description of the abject to a cruel woman. He explains to Robert that sometimes he has a tune in his head with English lyrics, and tells him that once he quarrelled with a woman and the whole time he was humming a tune, even when she shouted at him. Then when he left and got outside he remembered the lyrics—"I've got a woman, mean as she could be." All of this takes place against the sounds of guard dogs barking and shots being fired in the distance, imbricating different levels of masculinity and misogyny.

When he departs, Robert leaves a note for Bruno: "Everything has to change. So Long. R." Bruno reads it, says "I'll try" and tosses the paper into the wind, uttering something which is a cross between a war cry and a primal scream. Robert is seen, motionless at a station, exchanging his empty suitcase for an exercise book in which a young boy has written direct transcripts of what he has seen. It is a nostalgic and illusory gesture; Wenders describes the gaze of this child, sitting at the station doing his homework, as his dream of a film director, a reminder "with what curiosity and lack of prejudice it is possible to look at the world" (Wenders, 1997: 43). There are several closing shots of Bruno's truck and the train intercut, intersecting and, finally, divergent. In the last shot of the film Bruno sits in the passenger seat of the truck adjacent to a cinema which no longer shows films.

The failure to develop a border and a clear separation between self and object undermines the third space making it vulnerable to invasion or collapse. A fear of dependency upon the maternal has led Bruno to an unconscious dread of women and sexual intercourse, and an incapacity to defend himself against them (the last woman he encounters is middle-aged, in a cinema carrying out her father's wishes). He is left feeling marooned "inside", his affective capability arrested, incapable of effective symbolisation. So, he retreats to the interior of his truck/cinema museum—only on the road, in movement, is he guaranteed personal continuity. Cinema is his "father", the resource of the paternal narrative and the source of language, meaning and culture: the only defence against intrusion, anxiety, loss, abandonment and, above all, *powerlessness*.

Chapter 3

Traversing Identity: Home, Family and Gender in *Paris, Texas*

Writing in 1983 about Nicholas Ray's films, Wim Wenders describes the ways in which the English and American use of the word "home" covered much of what in German there are many words for: "building," "house," "family house," "home town," and so on (Wenders, 1989). A year later discussing the American dream, the director most closely identified with "road movies" locates what for him is the contradictory expression "mobile homes." The expression fascinates Wenders because it suggests somewhere you could be at home yet on the road at the same time; a mobile "belonging," not fixed anywhere.

Paris, Texas is a home movie and it is a road movie. Scene 60 features Super-8 footage of a holiday the five principal characters had three years prior to the diegetic time of the narrative (see Shephard and Wenders, 1983). The roads in the film are the old Route 66, the transcontinental freeway, and other, abandoned roads. The abandoned roads are sites of decay, wrecked cars, and memories absorbed by the desert: sites of loss. At one point early on, Travis leaves the highway and his brother finds him seated on a 1950s pick-up wreck. Initially, Travis is seen to lack directionality as he wanders off the main road or disappears from the motel, at this stage still straying on *excluded ground*:

[f]or the space that engrosses the deject, the excluded, is never *one*, nor *homogeneous*, nor *totalizable*, but essentially divisible, foldable and catastrophic. A deviser of territories, languages, works, the *deject* never stops demarcating his universe whose fluid confines—for they are constituted of a

non-object, the abject—constantly question his solidity and impel him to start afresh. A tireless builder, the deject is in short a *stray*. (Kristeva, 1982: 8)

Home is conventionally the location of family, homogeneous and totalizable; in the film only one actual home is shown. Significantly omitted from the final cut is what in the shooting script is the final scene. This scene has Travis in Paris, Texas, building a house on the plot of land he had purchased when he and his wife, Jane, and son, Hunter, were together: a home for his now "broken" family. He receives a mail delivery which contains Super-8 film of his son and his estranged wife. The footage has images of Hunter and Jane travelling across the country, passing the camera back and forth to each other. What we do not know is whether they are travelling towards or away from Travis. The use of the footage is one of many *distancing* motifs used throughout the film, part of the dialogue of fluidity and solidity. As I shall show, the final screen version has a very different ending—on the road, with Travis, the *stray* and *deject*, impelled to start afresh, but with no home in sight.

The home of Travis's brother, Walt, and his wife, Anne, is situated in Burbank, a suburb of Los Angeles close to Hollywood, and imaged in a way which suggests an "ideal" movie home. Even Anne and Walt's performance styles are studiedly restricted to the conventions of cinema discourse. Theirs is the only home and family in the primary narration. The trailer home of Travis and Jane is extra-diegetic. Only the child, Hunter, has lived in both spaces, although Travis stays for a while in the Burbank home. Walt (the name needs no comment) works in billboard advertising which confirms his home and family as being constructed from, and financed by, *images*. I stress these points at this stage because my discussion will focus on *home* and *family* in relation to the Symbolic Order and in gendered terms. The film works with a series of binary oppositions, although these are also commutable as many of the borders in the film are traversed. Burbank is the space of the literal (overliteral) home and the literal family—the place which the shot composition, editing, lighting and acting style suggest is delivered from all depth. Throughout the film there is also a focus on the figurative home and family—sites of dream and gendered fantasy.

My principal theoretical source for this analysis of *Paris, Texas* is Julia Kristeva's concept of *abjection* which is most fully articulated in *Powers of Horror*. The concept is described in a number of ways, but for my purposes I want to focus upon those definitions which refer to the way in which "the abject eludes the binary oppositions that structure the symbolic order" (Taylor, 1987: 159); such systems as "home" and "family" are constructed to exclude the heterogeneous abject which manifests itself in transgressive *positions*, on the borders of the binaries of Symbolic codings. The abject cannot be "integrated with a given system of signs" (Kristeva, 1982: 14). In Scene 106 Travis, speaking of himself in the third person to Jane in the Keyhole Club, says "[he] just ran. He ran until the sun came up and he couldn't run any further. . . . For five days, he ran like this until *every sign of man* had disappeared" (Shephard and Wenders, 1983: 180; my emphasis). The figure of Travis/traverse cannot himself be integrated with a system of signs, despite efforts to become *the* father and to restore the symbiosis of mother and child in the last scenes of the film. The whole film is overcoded, overloaded with "signs of man," the realm of the Symbolic Order. Kristeva argues that the social contract is based on an essentially sacrificial relationship of separation and articulation of differences which produce communicable meaning. This is offered as "natural" but it is a structure obscured in a sociohistorical context of Christian/western culture. The "west" in the film is not simply topographical, or generic, but refers also to a European/American system of discursive power—hence the ambiguity of Paris, Texas. A rejection of the Symbolic leads to a rejection of the paternal function and, ultimately, generates psychosis (Travis's "look" and his movements in the initial stages of the film suggest this). Abjection resists the intelligibility and signification of "home" and "family."

For Kristeva, abjection is very much concerned with boundary and border, the margin or limen which is "a void that is not nothing but indicates . . . a defiance or challenge to symbolisation" (Kristeva, 1982: 51). The border is the site of the binary, the locus of gender dichotomy with its links to forms of sexual violence. Ambivalence is the prevailing characteristic of the film and of abjection itself, "[t]he abject is, by definition, the sign of an impossible ob-ject, boundary and limit" (Kristeva,1982: 154). The title of the film announces boundary and division, a seemingly contradictory state, an *entre-deux*—never reducible to the differences it joins and separates (bonding and separation are themes which recur throughout). Travis tells Walt that their father used to introduce his wife as the girl he met in Paris, then pause for the punch line, "Texas." Later he tells Hunter that his father would look at his mother and he wouldn't see her, just an *idea* of her, that she came from Paris, France. Walt, by marrying a French woman, replicates this "idea." Travis is adamant, however, that his mother was not a "fancy woman," implying that Hunter's is, "*[m]y* mother, not *your* mother—my mother was not a fancy woman" (Shephard and Wenders, 1983: 168).

Linked with Kristeva's concept of the abject (invariably identified with the feminine, the improper and unclean "refuse" thrown away from the proper and clean family home) and abjection, elaborated through a failure to recognise its kin (Travis's situation when Walt first encounters him after a four-year absence), is the notion of "home" as defined by Biddy Martin and Chandra Mohanty. They develop their idea of home as containing at least

two specific modalities: being home and not being home. "Being home" refers to the place where one lives within familiar, safe, protected boundaries; "not being home" is a matter of realising that home was an illusion of coherence and safety based on the exclusion of specific histories of oppression and resistance, the repression of differences even within oneself. Because these locations acquire meaning and function as sites of personal and historical struggles, they work against the notion of an unproblematic geographic location of home. (Martin and Mohanty, 1988: 169)

Apart from the European/American division signified by the film's title, Paris, Texas is also a Polaroid photograph, a vacant lot and, for Travis, the idea that it is his place of conception—the place where his parents first were lovers. Except for the original shooting script, it has no geographic location in the narration of the film. For both Travis and Jane, but for differently gendered reasons, "not being home" is a refuge, an escape, a flight from illusions shaped by specific ideologies of oppression which neither of them can articulate abstractly but only existentially. In the Keyhole Club sequences, however, Travis does, at least, begin the discursive tracing of the reasons for his flight.

For Travis Paris, Texas, is the site prior to the *inaugural loss* which founds his socio-symbolic being. The abject is constituted as the "object" of primal repression anterior to, but within the breaches of, secondary repression—the entry into the Symbolic Order, the Word of the Father, language itself. Before this "entry" was the separation from the Mother—the space of the imprecise, uncertain and transgressive borders of the semiotic *chora*. For Kristeva the *speaking* subject is structured in the Symbolic Order by the separation from the Mother through the paternal agency which "introduces the symbolic division between 'subject' (child) and 'object' (mother)"(Kristeva, 1982: 44). The proper name, in psychoanalytic discourse, is always the name of the father. For Travis, this identification is compounded by sharing both first name and surname with his father. This is tied in with the linking of the father and death which I will refer to later.

The images at the opening of the film only stand alone in the strictly visual sense; they are not just situated in a physical, mappable landscape (Big Bend, Texas), but they are also images in a popular cultural landscape, both mythic and cinematic—the west of the frontier, and of the western genre. They are spatial and temporal images, shot accordingly, contextualised and contained simultaneously in both an old and a new web of meaning. Not only are the images historicised and genre located, but they are also *gendered*. *Paris, Texas* is about masculinity as an ideology articulated with the west, with the automobile, and with the road: located in the nineteenth century and the 1950s (cf. the 1958 Ranchero), at once epic and derelict—sidelined and obsolescent images. The opening evokes John Ford and John Wayne, but Travis is displaced, not a hero now but a modern American father and husband in suit, tie, and baseball cap (he later changes to a more cowboy style of dress). The key establishing activity is the border crossing, because the film is about crossing borders of patriarchy, of Europe/America. Wenders's America is a by-product of the European imagination: a series of "cultural imaginaries." (The film is, incidentally, a French/German co-production, and *not* American.)

A very obvious contrast is set up between the opening desert sequences with images of substance, lit in very specific ways, and the populated former desert of suburban Los Angeles—brightly lit, decontextualised images partly generated by the obviously named billboard maker, Walt. The body language, the framing and composition, and the performance styles all suggest a certain insubstantiality, and image barrenness (Anne and Walt cannot have a child). So, two movie cultural forms emerge and are contrasted: the western male, and the 1950s clean-cut, well-lit family romance. Both are off-centre (this can even be seen in an early reverse shot of Walt and Travis). Compared with the image-sequencing of relatively long takes of the opening segment of the film, the Burbank scenes feature shorter takes, speeding up and a sense of time-space compression. Wenders establishes what Cook calls "a duality of two worlds" (Cook and Gemünden, 1997: 123)—hyper-real and postmodern (cf. the biotechnical design of Walt's building in Glendale)—and what Baudrillard calls the archaic envelope of place, object, the adobe and myth. Houston, where the Keyhole Club sequences take place, is also hyper-real and postmodern—with its cold, rectangular and opaque bank—but also has its archaic envelopes: saloons, laundromats, and its empty epic western echoes.

The film begins, in the desert, by tracing the stages of birth in a space marked by the uncertainty of its borders, the "remaindered" wasteland of the abject. Throughout the film, Nature is seen as an opponent. All spaces are colonised by roads, cars, freeways, bridges, railroads, power lines, aeroplanes; there are few signs of earth or water as productive sites of fertility, but only of desertification and abandonment.

As the camera glides over a vast, empty landscape, Travis (unnamed and unknown at this point) is gradually pinpointed, "his lips are cracked and swollen and his tongue moves from side to side as though searching for moisture in the air" (Shephard and Wenders, 1983: 1). As if to underscore the significance of the landscape generically, he discards the empty water bottle of the male western convention. More important, when he arrives at a gas station on a remote highway, he goes directly to the water pipe, as if to suckle a breast, but it is dry. In the gas station store, he opens the fridge and, ignoring the six-packs of beer (because he is inscribed as an "infant" at this stage), grabs a handful of icecubes and starts eating the ice as he collapses. Later, when he enters into Language and becomes again a speaking subject, he tells Walt that when he was a baby his mother gave him icecubes to suck on when he was teething. What I am describing is a fairly obvious reenactment of the birth and nursing process—his body extricates itself, as being alive, from that border.

The collapse on the border (the doctor who is summoned asks him "[y]ou know which side a' the border yer on?") repeats the inaugural loss and separation. This occurs in the Terlingua (third language— neither American nor European? Language of the earth, the chthonic? Travis's middle name is Clay) Medical Clinic on the Mexican border. The script describes Travis as "marooned between some tragic event in his past and the helplessness of his present situation"; literally, the reference is to the flight from Jane four years ago and the present car crash; figuratively, it is to the process of expulsion or abjection. For all of the film, Travis remains "marooned between"—*entre-deux*. His bruised, unclean body dressed in an ambiguous class and ethnic mix of cheap Mexican suit and sun-bleached baseball cap has, ultimately, to be left behind by Travis as he rehearses his childhood stages in abbreviated, synoptic form. Initially, he is without language (preSymbolic) and when his brother, Walt, fetches him in a hired car, he sits in the back like a small child, rather than in the passenger's seat. He cries at one point, refuses to fly (he is still bound to the realm of the mother—the chthonic) and, when Walt returns to the car-hire lot, insists on having the same car. The attachment to the safe and the familiar and the vertiginous fear of the loss of boundaries are all recognisable symptoms of abjection. His movements are robotic, psychotic even—a *chiasmic* figure still. Walt calls him a "spoiled child" at one point, which, metaphorically, he is, of course, because of abjection.

In Kristeva's analysis, the abject is caused to exist by the logic of *exclusion*, the jettisoning of defilement (linked to the feminine) from the Symbolic system. That Travis is unable to live with Jane, takes flight across the Mexican border (his mother's maiden name was Spanish—Sequine) and disappears for four years is the result of a conflict between an imperfect belonging in the Symbolic Order and, what Kristeva calls, the weakness of prohibition which does not succeed in differentiating itself sufficiently from the *(m)other* but allows it to threaten one's own and clean self (we see Travis washed and shaved in the motel on another stage of his return to the Symbolic). Travis's body language, his gentle, uninflected voice and his relationship to his son (who, when describing space theories to him in Houston, and in his behaviour in the "buddy" sequences in the Broadway bar and in the laundromat, "fathers" him) all suggest an incompletely masculinized figure—almost a third gender, or third genre. The tearing of the child from the mother seems, in Travis's case, unfinished. Later, he says to Jane "it was me who tore you apart," as if to re-enact, or avenge even, his own inaugural loss and abjection.

Each stage of the film reintroduces Travis to the Symbolic Order. For example, initially he avoids the mirror in the motel room in his "silent" phase (presumably, he used it while shaving, but this is off-screen), but later he speeds up his growth, eats solid food at the diner, drives Walt's car, engages in conversation, watches the aircraft from his brother's home, walks past a van with an "Airborne" sign on it and, finally, leaves the ground (the chthonic) when he joins Walt on one of his billboard scaffolds. The latter enables him to tell Walt he is leaving, and, borrowing cash and credit cards, he rejoins the adult, male world and prepares to find a woman (Jane), completing the conventional symbolic trajectory. He has also learned from Walt that their mother had died while he was in "exile" out of America. The separation would seem complete.

At Walt's house, when Travis dresses up (in a bizarre melange of his own and his brother's clothes, rounded off with a Stetson) as *the* father, he looks at himself in a full-length mirror, acknowledging a successful traversing of the mirror-stage. Interestingly enough, he assembles his

image of *the* father (the definite article is stressed deliberately in the
script to emphasise the Symbolic) from *images* of the masculine in
magazines in the terms of the patriarchally constructed Hispanic maid
(third world woman identified with *cleaning*, and also perhaps with his
mother's Hispanic roots). Carmelita, the maid, asks him if he wants to
be a rich father or a poor father, telling him that "there is no in-
between." She also tells him he must look up at the sky and never at the
ground (linked with earth and the dirty feminine) and "you must walk
very stiff," completing the phallic imagery. Many such figures in the
film prepare Travis for the "real world," helping him in his quest to
"forget" abjection, but each one, in some way or other, is marked by
some trace of this unnameable—Walt shares the same mother, Anne is
from Paris and also "mothers" him as well as suggesting desire,
whereas Carmelita joins him in the Mexican songs he hums, as well as
having a function linked to the "dirty." However much the *exile*
ceaselessly seeks to separate himself from the abject, it is a *land of
oblivion* that is constantly remembered. In many ways, Paris, Texas,
signifies this land of oblivion—a primal scene—the place where Travis
imagines he was conceived. This attempt to rewrite reproduction under
his control and in his terms "fulfils the primal scene fantasy of being
present at the moment of one's conception" (Cohan and Hark, 1993:
247).

At the Burbank home Travis eats very little and sleeps not at all,
anxious to forestall the workings of the primary repression that opened
up the spaces of the unconscious, of dream—a realm of the semiotic
and of disruptive "pulsions." He is seen washing up and cleaning
endless numbers of shoes (at one point measuring his son's cowboy
boots against his own—a reminder of his wish to become the son), as a
way of maintaining his distance from the unclean feminine. His sister-
in-law Anne, contained within her stylised role as surrogate mother to
Hunter and, as one gesture shows, to Travis, also acts out a glimpsed
intertextual reference to *desire* as encoded in the cinematic trope of the
French "seductress"—the dangerous woman. In one scene, Travis and
Anne mirror each other precisely in reverse shot as they sit each with an
elbow on the table opposite each other; this shot further emphasises
Travis's incomplete identification with the masculine, Anne's role as
reflection of the masculine in the Symbolic Order, and Travis's
sublimated wish to enter the spaces of the feminine other. The shot also
shows, by its reverse angle, that she is not sufficiently *othered* perhaps.

As the "child" in Travis becomes chronologically a fully separated
being, the mother is still not adequately *forgotten*, which is why Anne

has to "disappear" from the narrative shortly after the reverse shot just
discussed, and why Jane never comes close to him again, her "danger"
screened by distance. Travis sees Jane behind the glass of her car
window, screened in the home movie, through the mirror in the
Keyhole club, and framed in the hotel window. Interestingly, the
windows of the Meridian hotel are shot in such a way as to suggest
endless television screens - one of many indications throughout of
overcoded, culturally mediated value.

Hunter has lived with Walt and Anne for three years ("given away"
by Jane at the point when Travis's mother dies), treating them as his
family and forgetting his "real" mother—watching the Super-8 footage,
he says "[t]hat's not her, that's only her in a movie . . . a long time, ago
. . . in a galaxy far, far away." In a sense, this shields him from the
pulsions of abjection, the Star Wars discourse effectively jettisoning her
to a great distance. He is surrounded by images of "the Name of the
Father," symbolic masculinity in the form of boys' toys, Star Wars,
NASA icons, the discourses of science and space travel. Unlike Travis,
he is firmly settled in the Symbolic Order of the father, a fixed and
model child surrounded by models: cars, planes, high technology. At
one point, referring to a car he says "it's a girl's car" (it's his mother's).
Walt and Anne, encoding and embodying for Hunter the *middle class*
home and family (but always offered as universal) and living in and off
the Symbolic Order literally and figuratively, provide a clean, suburban
(remote from the desert) family home where the child as speaking
subject is "at home" in the patriarchal, living within familiar, safe,
protected boundaries, unaware of the repression of differences.

Travis's presence opens up ambiguities (Hunter tries to explain to a
friend that he has two fathers, but gives up; he also tells Travis that he
could always feel him walking around and talking someplace when he
had disappeared) and threatens Anne and Walt (who is unable to father
a child biologically) for the first time with the spectre of "not being at
home". Their space, their lifestyle, their speech and their body language
are all precise, boundaried, and framed by the logic of *exclusion*. With
them, Hunter would grow untroubled by the memory of abjection,
always "at home" in the world. At the same time, however, the growth,
insight and, possibly, creative awareness that Travis achieves (in the
sense that he is able to construct a narrative of abjection) would also be
denied him. As Kristeva shows, abjection has a double effect as it is a
time both of oblivion and revelation. Travis's motives in restoring
Hunter to Jane are, therefore, complex and ambiguous. Partly it is to
renew the Madonna/child story, partly to put together the dyadic unity

he has torn apart, but also it is to overcome his own separation from the mother, as well as, perhaps, to open up a more *provisional* sense of identity for Hunter to challenge and defy the stable essences of the Symbolic.

The Super-8 home movie shows Travis in cowboy hat, Hunter "driving," and Jane dancing (Monroe-like) *on her own* away from the family group, circling round and round. These are all, potentially, "undomesticated" images, markers of flight and mobility, yet contained within the frame of the *home* movie. It is also a *silent* movie. Anne and Walt are shown in more static and self-conscious poses.

The footage seems to help Hunter work out something of his ambiguous location. To both men, he says "Goodnight, Dad" and, later, in what looks like a silent movie routine he mimics Travis's actions when they walk home from school, separate but parallel; later, on the road, they wear similar clothes. However, the Super-8 film also prefigures the Keyhole scenes where Travis and Jane discursively trace the course of their own separation, loss of home, and breakup of family. At the same time, Anne is afraid what will happen to her marriage if they lose Hunter, and accuses Walt of promoting "all this father-son business." It is as if Anne senses that she is to become the site of abjection, the remaindered maternal body, which has been kept at bay by her clean home and suburban family. Identity, system, order are all disturbed as borders, positions and rules are brought into question by the in-between, the ambiguous and the composite. She is reminded that Hunter is not kin and that the familiar (the space of *the* family) and the safe are imperilled.

When Anne says she loves Hunter like her own flesh and blood, while Walt insists that Travis *is* his father, Hunter *is* his son, questions are raised about biological essentialism as the only model of family available for a complex number of socio-cultural reasons, but for Walt (*image* man) it is the only model because it is a *model*, constructed within the hegemonic discourse and endorsed by the advertising and movie industries.

After a long series of interior scenes (women are rarely placed in exterior shots) Travis decides to search for Jane based upon information supplied by Anne. The "home movie" becomes a "road movie" again as Travis buys a used Ranchero (perhaps an echo of the pick-up he crashed earlier) and, equipped with binoculars and walkie-talkies, he takes Hunter on a rite of passage to track Jane down. Travis resumes (in both senses of the word) some of his "forgotten" masculinity as he and his son, in an extended "buddy movie" sequence, stake out the (m)other in a mock thriller scenario. Each month at the same time Jane banks money for Hunter in Houston, so they are able to locate and close in on her—as *hunters*—trailing her to her place of work. In a phone call to Walt, Hunter describes the Ranchero as "a real family car" with emphasis on the "family," but equally it could have been on the "real." Significantly, they drive across the desert as though, in returning Hunter to his mother, Travis is trying not only to bridge the four-year gap but, in reprising the earlier sequences of the film with him and Walt in the car, is also putting the child through the birth/separation symbolisation stages. As I have said previously, a lot of Hunter's discourse and behaviour is "adult" paternal in these scenes. He has a grasp of the dominant discourse of technological complexity and theories of creation unknown to his "borderline" male father; he is also the first to spot Jane, while Travis dozes, and it is he who tells his father which way to turn in the pursuit.

Prisoners of Gender

In the chapter in *Looka Yonder* called "Sam Shephard's Cowboy Mouth," Duncan Webster refers to Travis and Jane as "prisoners of gender" (Webster, 1988). It is this phrase which I want to explore and, hopefully, trace culturally. *Paris, Texas* is, at many levels, concerned with gender fundamentalism—with divisions, icons, discourses which have come to inhabit individuals as though they were natural. They constitute an artificial territoriality but exist ideologically as part of an unreflexive design/model for the male, repressing continuous relations with the mother. At the simplest level Travis's clothes, the Ranchero pick-up, the drinking set-piece in the saloon, the technology, the buddy imagery, the son's name, the highway, the Red River and other intertextual references, the imaging of women in two-dimensional frames (in the gas station store at the beginning, on the dismantled billboard, as well as in the Keyhole sequences) and the road movie/western signs, and the Mojave desert (the site for atom bomb testing and development) all contribute towards a masculinist discourse. In other words, the highly charged visual/iconic landscape is not simply an empirical/geographical fact but a culturally loaded and gendered space—violence is not simply the subject of the text but part of the syntax of the narrative. At this point in the film Travis and Hunter enter what Kristeva calls men's time, or linear time—time as project, teleology, departure, progression and arrival. Early in the film Walt tells Travis he is too busy to drive and needs to take a plane. Men's time is also that of Language, enhanced by the use of the walkie-talkies which give them power over the silent, pursued woman—preverbal.

The desert silence—prior to language—is the site of what Kristeva defines as the semiotic *chora*, an essentially mobile and extremely provisional articulation (uncertain and indeterminate), as opposed to a *disposition* that already depends on social, experiential constraints and on representation. Nevertheless the Symbolic, the disposing of the subject through language in gender, time and space, functions in a dialogical relationship with the semiotic; each is a condition of the other. For Kristeva "the territory of the maternal is not a space confined to biological characteristics; it is the position a subject, any subject, can assume towards the symbolic order" (Furman, 1985: 73). This positioning becomes culturally axiomatic; it fixes and reduces, but it is also subject to rupture—for example, Hunter's disgust at Travis's drunkenness in the saloon and his androgynous looks, yet in the laundromat he watches a John Wayne movie.

The *chora* precedes and underlies figuration and specularization. Jane and the other women in the Keyhole Club are forced into positions of specularity—they can see only themselves, not the men—they exist solely in symbolic configuration, subject to the language of command and masculine fantasy. This is because the semiotic connects and orients the body to the mother through "drives" (energy discharges); the semiotized body is a place of permanent scission, a space, not an essence, of discontinuities and anarchies. The maternal body mediates the Symbolic law organising social relations—home and family, for instance—and becomes the ordering principle of the semiotic *chora* which is on the path of destruction, aggression and death (compare Travis's relations with Jane after she becomes a mother, and her struggle against symbolisation). The semiotic continuum must be split if signification is to be produced, and this is at the heart of the film's deeply conflicted narrative around home and family—Walt and Anne represent that "split" and disappear when the semiotic intercedes.

The last quarter of the film focuses upon Travis, Jane and Hunter. This part of the film is concerned with tracing the sources of the loathing and violence which has sundered images of home and family. The heterogeneous flux cannot inhabit the fixity of the hom(e)ogeneous, and abjection threatens famil(iarit)y. These scenes highlight the instability of the Symbolic function, in what Kristeva calls its most significant aspect, the ban placed on the body of the maternal. The extended revelation scenes in the Keyhole Club (site of the voyeur and fantasist) between Jane and Travis take "the ego back to its source on the abominable limits from which, in order to be, the ego has broken away—it assigns it a source in the non-ego, drive and death. Abjection is a resurrection that has gone through death (of the ego)" (Kristeva, 1982: 15). It is also described by Kristeva as a kind of *narcissistic crisis*. Women are constantly treated in the film as the *limit* or borderline which is why in the Keyhole Club men are heavily screened from them by mirror, telephone, and "invisibility," anything but *immediacy*.

The past relationship between Travis and Jane is discursively and obliquely related by Travis, speaking of himself and her in the third person, "I knew these people . . .these two people" (Kristeva refers at one point in *Powers of Horror* to the *stray* considering himself as equivalent to a third party). The location is a club predicated upon female passivity and commodification, with women domesticated in various stereotypical interiors and arranged in set poses for the male gaze, but not the touch. The woman does not return the gaze, because the mirrors in the booths only permit the men to see. To speak his violence and his love Travis turns his back on the mirror, as Jane, discursively, becomes "the untouchable, impossible, absent body of the mother" in this moment of "narcissistic perturbation" which is also the revelation referred to above. For the speaking being—almost monosyllabic until this point—it is the moment:

that secondary repression, with its reserve of symbolic means, attempts to transfer to its own account, which has thus been overdrawn, the resources of primal repression. The archaic economy is brought into full light of day, signified, verbalised. Its strategies (rejecting, separating, repeating/abjecting) hence find a symbolic existence, and the very logic of the symbolic— arguments, demonstrations, proofs etc.—must conform to it. It is then that the abject ceases to be circumscribed, reasoned with, thrust aside: it appears as abject. (Kristeva, 1982: 15)

The trailer life of the couple corresponds precisely with this, and the revelation narrative gives it symbolic existence.

Initially, as described by Travis, Jane in her late teens and he in his late thirties/early forties (the paternal metaphor suggests itself) enjoy an idyllic, romantic love. For reasons he cannot understand, he loved her more than he felt possible and even gave up work to be home with her. However, he describes himself as starting to get "kind of torn inside"— reentering the space of inaugural loss, primary separation, the splitting of the subject inscribed in the Symbolic Order. The literal impossibility of origin, of return, to the "ever-absent body of the mother" renders desire insatiable. This accounts for his jealousy, possessiveness, violence, drunkenness, and enslavement of Jane—he needs her to be unclean, defiled, unfaithful. When she becomes pregnant, Jane, as mother enchained to the Symbolic Order, dreams of escape from their mobile home. There is no space for the feminine in the film's symbolisation except in the domestic or the reclining, passive pose of the billboard or the pin-up calendar (there is space in Kristeva's theory for the feminine in the Symbolic, by detaching the mother function from the specificities of gender). Travis tied a cowbell to Jane's ankle (downgrading her from the human and recalling the masculine ranch of the western genre) so he could hear her at night if she tried to get out of bed. In his turn, Travis wished he was far away, lost in a deep, vast country where nobody knew him—somewhere without language or streets. He dreamed about this place without knowing its name. Within the Symbolic it is *unnameable*; Kristeva names it as the *chora*, the maternal body.

Speaking of a non-western hunter society, Peggy Reeves Sanday describes fear, conflict and strife:

In these societies, males believe that there is an uncontrollable force that may strike at any time and against which men must be prepared to defend their integrity. The nature of the force and its source are not well defined, but often they are associated with female sexuality and reproductive functions. Men believe it is their duty to harness this force, to prevent chaos and to maintain equilibrium. They go to extraordinary lengths to acquire some of the power for themselves so that they will not be impotent when it is time to fight. Men attempt to neutralise the power they think is inherent in women by stealing it, nullifying it, or banishing it to invisibility. (Sanday, 1981: 164)

This, from an anthropological perspective, complements Kristeva's psychoanalytical approach by tracing the instability of the unitary male subject and the need to harness female sexuality to an extent that desire becomes mutated into the desire for violence against the very source of desire itself. Both writers are not simply talking about men and women, but about concepts and principles which constitute the "feminine" by exclusion from the realm of value. Numerous cultural spaces are rendered off-limits to women as they are confined to obedient dependency. The Symbolic Order establishes cultural patterns which make the male functionally complete, but this is always a provisional "completeness" and Travis needs Jane to "fill up his emptiness." Jane refuses to use Hunter to do this for her which is why she gives him to Anne and Walt.

In an attempt to achieve some space and power, Jane burns down the trailer and escapes with the child. In the Freudian scenario, as well as having connotations of purification, fire is associated with male sexuality (Travis ties her to a stove), and perhaps Jane is trying to recover some "mastery" by her action, but in non-western cultures fire is often identified with shamanic power and magic. In Dobu society, the mythical origin of fire is from the vagina of an old woman, and it is women who are thought to have the power of flight (Eliade, 1989). Whatever the significance, the fire precipitates the flight which leads to Travis's four-year disappearance.   Mother, lover, other, Jane is idealised as representing the space of the semiotic for Travis, denying the psychic pain and violence (the staging of separation) which characterises the interaction between her and Hunter.   Unable to "forget" his own inaugural loss which rends and tears him, he sentimentalises the mother-child symbiosis through his paternal agency as a way of forestalling the mirror stage and restoring the undifferentiated being of the *chora*. Perhaps Hunter is unconsciously doing the same when, in the Meridian Hotel, in his mother's embrace he mimes the cutting of her hair to make the two of them identical.

The only inclusive spaces for a woman in the socio-symbolic stratum are as wife and mother in the home and the family: for male, read mobile, for female, home. For Jane these discourses of gendered power demobilise and exclude her affective life *as a woman* and her condition as a social being. In response, she counter-invests the violence she has endured as the only form of *agency* available to her—the burning of the trailer renders it neither mobile nor home.   Her "independence" as a worker in the Keyhole Club—she switches the light on and off, the clients cannot touch her, nor does she see them—is, of course, a deeply conflicted freedom (there is a large mural of the Statue of Liberty on an exterior wall of the club as well as some racist graffiti) as she performs in yet another permitted discursive space as the object of male sexual fantasies; every man, she tells Travis, has his voice.

Throughout the film, we see Travis giving birth to himself as an I by "abjecting the mother's body." However, there is considerable instability of both fathering and mothering as I have argued, and it is this instability—that which does not respect borders, positions, rules— which renders the home unhomely (*unheimlich*) and the family unintelligible. Undisturbed and unambiguous, identity, system and order —the realm of the Symbolic—can deliver both home and family. Ironically, it is the confrontation with the feminine—the maternal body, conventionally the em-bodi-ment of home and family—that brings the abject back in "fleeting encounters." McAfee describes these encounters as "fleeting" because "we flee, horrified of falling back into the maternal body, where no difference—and thus no subjectivity—is possible" (McAfee, 1993: 118). Horrified, yes, but also fascinated. With his compulsion to repeat, Travis is drawn to the uncanny—the buried and repressed—the *unheimlich*.

In a sense, the Keyhole sequences are an example of what Alice Jardine calls *gynesis*—the putting of women into discourse. Almost silent throughout, Jane (or an idea of Jane) is constructed both as a model for the unknowable and as a figure who dominates Travis's desire, which he resents (hence the violence) yet is contained by. She is both "screen goddess" (the cinematic aspects of the sequences are obvious, as are the confessional, prison visiting and analyst/analysand analogies) and "whore" in a pornography club. Jane is the site of nostalgia (for the maternal body), utopia, and misogyny.

As Papastergiadis points out in *Modernity as Exile* (1993), both the past and self-identity (for the exile, which Travis has been in a sense) begin with separation from the mother-tongue/country and discontent with the law of the father: "[h]e lies with his head between her legs . . . Everything here is re-enactment, everything here is return. Home is the return to where distance did not yet count" (Papastergiadis, 1993: 144). As I have argued, *Paris, Texas* is centrally concerned with reenactment and return, as was Travis's "exile" to the spaces of his mother's roots (her father was Spanish) south of the Mexican border. The frequent use of Hispanic reference in word and image and the Mexican songs and music rupture and puncture the growth away from the maternal and "remember" abjection.

The "homes" Travis returns to in the film are places where distance does not count. However, the composition of numerous shots indicates indirectness, screening and distance —the Super-8 movie; the mirror and telephone in the Keyhole Club; the gaps between Hunter and Travis walking home from school, in the Ranchero where the child mostly travels in the back (at one point, sitting next to his father in the cab he falls asleep on his shoulder and Travis gently detaches him), in the Broadway saloon bar and in the use of walkie-talkies and the discussions on NASA and space exploration; the gaps between brother, sister-in-law and Travis; and the contrast between the close-up on Hunter and Jane in the Meridian Hotel and the long shot of Travis watching from afar.

Giving up work so he could be close to Jane, confusing love with possession, and yet also alienating her, attaching a cowbell to her and tying her up to a stove are all symptoms of his attempts to construct a "home" where distance did not count. Endlessly seeking a territory, he is "reterritorialized on almost anything—memory, fetish or dream . . . [looking for] [w]hat will restore an equivalent of territory, valid as a home" (Deleuze and Guattari, 1994: 68, 69). Yet the paradox of the mobile home, unfixed and capable of distances, and their age gap, even, underscore his ambivalent position. This is to say nothing of the distances travelled in the "road movie" sections of the film, the railroad tracks and the interstate which take the time of the city to the space of the desert and domesticate it. The ultimate, originary, distance from the mother, of course, determines Travis's final decision to leave Jane and Hunter again.

Metaphorically, he restores the distance between himself and his mother by bringing Jane and Hunter together again in the hotel. The composition of this sequence uses shots which close the distance between mother and child literally (they embrace and circle round and round in a movement both maternal and erotic—prior to abjection) and figuratively by focusing on Hunter from angles which suggest progressively the three year old, the five year old, and, finally, the almost eight year old. It is Madonna and child, and yet also the *prohibited* love scene. At the end of the Keyhole sequence Travis turns the light on his face, and Jane switches off her light. This reverses the mirror and she sees his face. He sees the reflection of his face framed by her hair and body. The image has a gender-crossing, transgressive effect—he enters her as the maternal body, thus reversing the mirror-stage. The image also looks like Hunter with soft, androgynous looks and longer, blonde hair. It is the only "family" portrait of the present (Travis has an old Polaroid from the past), but it is also only an *image*. The three never close the distance between them.

Travis cannot live, as paternal agency, in that proximity ("with his head between her legs") but only in the distance that separates him. The final shot of the film has him driving away onto the freeway, complete with cowboy hat, into the "sunset" of neon-lit, nighttime Houston—the borderlander, forever marginalised by the cultural closures of the Symbolic. He passes a billboard (made by Walt?) with the final, ironic appropriation of love discourse, "TOGETHER WE MAKE IT HAPPEN—Republic Bank." Travis has reunited Jane and Hunter by locating her at a bank, where she deposits money received in exchange for fulfilling male fantasies. It would take another chapter to consider the extent to which the economy of desire is related to the Symbolic Order and the cultural dimensions of American finance capital. "Together," that home and family word, is stripped of all but its use as image.

I have mentioned the spatial gaps between Hunter and Travis. One scene which emphasises this is the one where Hunter, framed as an extension of a television set in the hotel room (fully integrated with signs and the mediated), listens to a tape-recorded message from Travis:

You belong together with your mother. It was me that tore you apart. And I owe it to you to bring you back together. But I can't stay with you. I could never heal up what happened. It's like a gap. But it left me alone in a way that I'll never get over. And right now I'm afraid. I'm afraid of walking away again. I'm afraid of what I might find. But I'm even more afraid of not facing this fear. I love you Hunter. I love you more than my life. (Shephard and Wenders, 1983: 185)

Apart from echoing the "together" of the billboard, Travis is speaking "in the name of *the* Father," of symbolisation; but he is also speaking of his own abjection ("gap") and separation—"walking away." Because of what Nietzsche calls "creative forgetting," Travis can hardly remember the presymbolic *chora*. In order to complete his reenactment and return to the Symbolic Order, he has to walk away from the scene of primal repression which he has staged in the Meridian (*entre-deux*) Hotel. This scene is "a void which is not nothing but designates . . . a defiance or challenge to symbolisation" (Kristeva, 1982: 51). The "fear" he speaks of is of the abject, as, in Kristeva's terms, the object of his phobia has no object but the abject, "that otherness, a burden both repelling and repelled. A deep well of memory that is inaccessible and intimate" (Kristeva, 1982: 6).

Travis's fear of the untouchable, impossible/absent body of the mother means that he can only survive in the Symbolic Order by confronting that otherness which, for him, is configured in Jane. Nevertheless, this confronting is only oblique and, in a sense, on his terms—for it is he who tells "their" story. His attraction to Jane, initially, is that she is very young (seventeen) and, therefore, closer to the age of his mother at his own conception. Anne, his peer and not a mother (Walt says she could only have children with another man; *he* "fathers" images) represents a different *otherness* —a possible space for feminine desire in the Symbolic Order—but Travis is unable to respond to her, literally as his brother's wife and figuratively because he is still burdened by that "deep well of memory that is unapproachable and intimate: the abject." In a sense, Anne does "give" him a family by providing clues as to the whereabouts of his child/wife and "releasing" his son.

At the Borders of the Unnameable

Throughout the film Travis has to work out his bearings while in the process of his return journey, but, as Jane Gallop argues, "the mother as mother is lost forever. . . . The mother as womb, homeland, source and grounding for the subject is irretrievably past" (Gallop, 1985: 53), hence no home is ever possible as "the subject is . . . in a foreign land, alienated." The "home movie" *has* to become a "road movie" as Travis will never "arrive":

The journey is a search for a centre, which has overcome any contestation with the peripheries, it is an "ideal" centre which knows of no outside and so can be composed only of an inside which is total and complete in itself. It is by virtue of such a centre/home [the Keyhole Club for the male, perhaps?]—both abstract and concrete—that identities can ever be rendered in a static and absolute form. But it is also by virtue of its abstraction that such a centre/home is never attainable. (Papastergiadis, 1993: 170)

The identities of Walt and Anne are rendered in a static and absolute form—their "ideal" centre/home is shot almost entirely in interior scenes—but as Walt "hands over" Hunter to Travis, and Anne yields information about Jane to him, they both cease to have substantive existence and are only represented, at a distance, by a collect call. They have served their purpose as agents of symbolisation—surrogate parents to Hunter and Travis—and the unitary status of home and family is uprooted. Incidentally, all the positive scenes between father and son are exterior ones, except after the showing of the Super-8 footage, and when Hunter "mothers" his drunken father in the laundromat.

Travis's leaving of Burbank re-enacts his earlier leaving of America and Jane's leaving of the trailer. Jane's flight, ultimately, leads her to the site/sight of the male voyeur, structured in the booths of patriarchy. Travis's journey, however, traces what Kristeva calls the death of the name of the father: "The exile cuts all links, including those that bind him to the belief that the thing called life has a meaning guaranteed by the dead father. For if meaning exists in the state of exile, it nevertheless finds no incarnation, and is ceaselessly produced and destroyed in geographical and discursive transformations. Exile is a way of surviving in the face of the dead father" (Kristeva, 1987: 298).

Travis's father died in a car crash, and in a scene cut from the film, there is a "vision" of Travis's own car crash shot from a subjective point of view seen through the windshield of a pick-up truck. The car is driving at an insane speed as if the driver were drunk. The car veers off the road and continues "its *suicidal path* towards rocks and a ravine" (Shephard and Wenders, 1983: 70; my emphasis). It would be possible to see the whole film as *both* an attempt to erase the father and a *suicidal path*—the drive towards death. In *Desire in Language* (1980) Kristeva, referring to Beckett's *First Love*, talks about a man experiencing love and simultaneously putting it to the test on the death of his father. Travis's father dies before his exile (the mother dies during it, unknown to him): his own car crash occurs while he is "missing" in the *land of oblivion*. Kristeva says that racked between the *father* and *Death* a man has a hard time finding something else to love. He could hardly venture in that direction, she suggests, unless he were confronted with an undifferentiated woman, tenacious and silent, preferably a prostitute. In the Keyhole Club booth, Jane becomes that undifferentiated woman, passive and silent, performing for men in exchange for money.

It is in this context that Travis is able to articulate the violence and domination which has destroyed their primary love relationship (as well as reenacting it in the booth exchanges), yet is facing Jane—who cannot see him—in what Kristeva calls *banishment love*. Banishment is above/beyond a life of love because "*to love* is to survive paternal meaning" (Kristeva, 1980: 150) . However, by reenacting his entry into the Symbolic throughout the film Travis is actually establishing a relationship with the world in the image, figuratively speaking, of the dead father:

Through this opening, he might look for woman. But the Other, the third-person father, is not that particular dead body. It is Death: it always was. It is the meaning of the narrative of the son, who never enunciated himself, save for and by virtue of this stretched out void of paternal Death, as ideal and inaccessible to any living being as it might seem. As long as a son pursues meaning in a story or through narratives, even if it eludes him, as long as he persists in his search he narrates in the name of Death for the father's corpses. (Kristeva, 1980: 150/1)

Travis's extended Keyhole narrative, his first significant "enunciation" in the film, is such a pursuit of meaning, and this is something which is achieved through the editing in the Keyhole sequences. This segment occupies almost one-sixth of the whole film's running time and is placed very close to the end. At this stage, we would expect perhaps a speeding up in the pace of the film, but instead Wenders slows it right down: there are only twenty six shots in the segment, with a number of fairly long takes. The editing creates a graphic conflict between colour qualities. Wenders follows the conversation of Travis and Jane by cutting from the client's side of the glass to the performer's. The scene reprises visually their earlier relationship which we only hear about through their respective narratives. Although both people are visible in most of the shots, the cutting stresses their separation by harsh colour contrasts. Jane's light-blue, almost washed-out stage setting, as seen from Travis's side of the glass clashes with the blackness and aluminium-foil reflections in the next shot. Jane is, initially, not specific but a generic woman, highly lit in an artificial and male-constructed interior location. Travis, similarly, is not only a specific man but a generic *man* (every man, Jane says, has his voice), underlit, obscure, the architect of the unreturnable gaze. The initial perspective is his. The breakthrough and breakdown occurs at two points, when Travis turns away from the mirror symbolically refusing the male gaze, and when he turns the light on his face and Jane turns off her light. This reverses the mirror and she sees his face. He sees the reflection of his face framed by her hair and body. As stated earlier, the image has a gender-crossing, transgressive effect—the dismantling of two long-sustained and separated gender ideologies of the woman and the man.

The last scenes take us finally from image to narrative, from silence to speech, from the ontological insecurities of masculinist violence to the dismantling of a maleness-centred western myth; throughout another set of silences, the lost highway of an artificially lit neon sunset. Out of place and out of time, Travis is incapable of loving either as husband or father.

The final scene (originally Travis was to be in Paris, Texas building a house for Jane and Hunter) had, for Wenders, "a liberating effect: there was a feeling which I knew would have consequences for my next film. The last shot as Travis leaves: I let him disappear in my own way, and all my previous male characters went with him. They have all taken up residence in a retirement home on the outskirts of Paris, Texas" (quoted in Cook and Gemünden, 1997: 128). It is very much a valedictory film: an epitaph to a certain model and ideology of maleness. Travis's journey has been in search of his own conception, the origins of his own autobiographical narrative: what he discovers, and is finally able to reflect upon, is that identity is not individual but interactive, socially and culturally formed, historically and ideologically gendered. His father's name is Travis (traverse), his son's name is Hunter (another piece of the archaic envelope), who is already into space age, hi-tech maleness ("a girl's car"). The forward movement is also a backward movement in a sense: "The entire film is needed to extract the alienated male hero from the central subject position of the narrative" (Cook and Gemünden, 1997: 129). One of the central problems is the erosion of psychic depth. Travis's loss of identity is attributed to a culture which he inhabits and which inhabits him, that reproduces images with increasing autonomy, irrespective of its own history: dissolution into isolated signifiers.

Although the main thrust of my argument has concentrated upon the impossibility of home and the unintelligibility of the family in respect of the prohibited maternal body, it should be remembered that not only does Travis not have his "own" name but his father's, that Hunter's nomination is collapsed phonemically in the father (Hunter/Hender son, even more pronounced in American English) and also that Travis "dies" twice for his son, once after the fire and then after the mother-son bonding in the Meridian. This suggests that Hunter will be caught in the spiral of abjection (metaphorically separating again from the mother) and the search that narrates in the name of Death.   The relocation of mother and son in a scene of mutuality is overdetermined by the absence of the paternal. At one point in the Meridian scene, the camera shows Jane swinging Hunter round and tilting him towards the window (they are several floors up) as if to jettison him. Even at the material level, how will Jane support Hunter economically, and how appropriate is her *unclean*, male-designated work, which would doubtless have to continue in the absence of any other maintenance, for this role?

In his search for the lost territory of the mother (significantly he throws away the Polaroid of the vacant lot while drinking in the Broadway saloon near the end), Travis seeks to overcome "the unthinkable of death by postulating maternal love in its place —in the place and stead of death and thought. This love . . . is perhaps a recall, on the near side of early identifications, of the primal shelter that ensured the survival of the newborn" (Kristeva, 1987: 177). He draws upon a discourse on ideal motherhood by reconstituting in the Meridian (and watching over it from a distance) the primal shelter of the bond between mother and child (it is, we notice, a *hotel*, a quasi-home—the space of "flight"). The whole film, as has been shown, is a "recall."

Both mother and child are figuratively reborn, Jane's wet hair confirming this. For Travis it is both a return to meaning and, simultaneously, a loss as he departs on his final drive (coded in the terms of the western) to Death (?), surrounded by the highway. Unlike Kolker and Beicken (1993), I do not see Travis finding "redemption in a new beginning"—the pain of loss is too sharp in the final shot— although I agree that he has achieved a significant level of understanding.

The film ends on an ambiguous note (the separated male on the open road), but I would interpret this as an indicator of the obsessed man, perhaps no longer so driven by the disruptive pulsions of abjection but fortified with the assumption of Death (his first exile had been a "mock" death), driving away from the woman and child (substituting for the father) to devote himself to his own "slow descents again, the long submersion" (Kristeva, 1980: 152), of pursuing the meaning of the narrative of the son. It is in this sense a sacrificial ending, as Travis stands in, metaphorically, for his own son ("I love you more than my life") to enable him to survive paternal meaning.

Travis remains in the fundamental condition of abjection, heading for the boundary (again) between subject and object, the borderlands of the *entre-deux*, the cultural origins of the patriarchal west (Paris and Texas, and the western), "[a] voyager in a night whose end flees" (Kristeva, 1982: 8). He is still the subject-in-process, confronting a relation of *alterity* within. The nearer he gets to the border the closer he is to the site of inaugural loss, the boundary between the *chora* and the Symbolic—the not-being-at-home of the *unheimlich*. Even if this state may prefigure an opening into the new, "the *Unheimliche* requires just the same the impetus of a new encounter with an unexpected outside element: arousing images of death, automatons, doubles, or the female sex, . . . uncanniness occurs when the boundaries between *imagination* and *reality* are erased" (Kristeva, 1991: 188).

In other words, the threats to identity are expelled *momentarily*, not deleted (this other form of erasure—between *imagination* and *reality* —is always present). The threats persist within the unitary status of the Symbolic as unsettling reminders, thresholds of instability threatening fixed boundaries, indicating that identity formation is a never-ending traversing, a dialogical rhythm. Not only is the feminine exiled from the Symbolic (however she may be domesticated, or "homed") and banned from the transgressive (unless passively serving it), but the masculine—the name of the father—is also/always journeying:

The country from which we come is always the one to which we are returning. You are on the return road which passes through the country of children in the maternal body. You have already passed through here: you recognise the landscape.   You have always been on the return road.   Why is it that the maternal landscape, the heimisch, and the familiar become so disquieting? The answer is less buried than we might suspect. The obliteration of any separation, the realisation of the desire which in itself obliterates a limit; all that which in effecting the movement of life in reality allows us to come closer to a goal, the short cuts, the crossing accomplished especially at the end of our lives; all that which overcomes, shortens, economises and assures satisfaction appears to affirm the life forces. All of that has another face turned towards death which is the detour of life. The abbreviating effect which affirms life asserts death (Cixous, 1976: 544).

The "road movie" in *Paris, Texas* is a return road movie, but the family/familiar is no longer *heimlich* but unsettling because the attempts to overcome separation, to e-*limin*-ate borders, and the abbreviating effect of the speeded-up reenactment of the child/man stages of development are all "economies" which signal death.   For Travis, arrival has always to be deferred if he is to survive.

All of Wenders's work engages with the ways in which Modernity confronts the affirmations of identity, relationships, home and family. If, as John Berger claims, migration is the quintessential condition of the twentieth century, then both home and family are less to do with houses and the small, biologically linked groupings of our establishment and media ideologies and more to do with mental/cultural constructs of ever-renewable *belongings* and deep, communal, but shifting mutualities. Wenders works with allegory and fantasy but, above all, with metaphor, as defined by Kristeva, "in so far as it gives form to the infantile psychic inscriptions situated at the borders of the unnameable" (Kristeva, 1992: 75).

Chapter 4

Borderline Identities and the Experience of the Stranger

In many of his films prior to *Wings of Desire* (1987) Wenders focused on representations of masculinity which confirmed the Symbolic Order but did not conform with its criteria of gendered roles: the uninhabitable spaces of home, family and work. These male representations are the road, the journey, the way of the nomadic: a shifting, itinerant regime of absences—mother, father, woman, child. It is a world of the dislocated, strangers and missing persons. The road is always open, a mental/cultural state as well as an actual location. Mobility is the key trope. There was, in some instances, a bonding in these films but, for the most part, the emphasis was on the individual male seeking some form of redemption in movement itself.

With *Wings of Desire* attention shifts to a city, a generation of strangers living out, and living in, the empty spaces and absent memories of post-war Germany. The film is a meditation on history, loss, forgetting and the possibility of desire, but it is a desire heavily shaded by the iconic presence of fascism. All of the three films dealt with in this chapter are concerned with reconciliation, healing, ethical virtue and developing a culture of mutuality out of alienation, borderline identities and monetised relations. The films are full of people "running away" but they are also "running towards". What they are running towards is never finally specified—it is the process itself which matters. These films are works of *revaluation* in many senses of the word. In *Faraway, So Close!* (1993), particularly, money is seen as the source of all acknowledged value—its currency, circulation and exchange determining all other relationships. Figuratively speaking, angels, children, storytellers and other agents of creativity are all marginalised, but in their marginality and otherness there is the potential for symbolic and ethical value, for forms of reparative love.

Berlin in *Wings of Desire* and *Faraway, So Close!* is the localised site where all have become potential strangers; a situation now intensified by the post-1989 international situation in which Berlin is also a *symptomatic* city. In *Until the End of the World* (1991) "missing persons" are in a line of flight across endless borders, empty time zones and image-identical metropolitan cities, their meanings constructed out of their uprootedness, their absence from *place*, or deterritorialization. Deterritorialization is a feature of most of Wenders's films but, recently, figures are seeking to be re-territorialized, looking for what will restore an equivalent of territory, valid as a home.

It is the phrase 'an equivalent of territory' which I wish to develop as a way of understanding the ethical and the cooperative in these films for, as Kristeva says in *Strangers to Ourselves* (Kristeva, 1991), we shall never be able to live at peace with the strangers around us if we are unable to tolerate the *otherness* in ourselves. Wenders's characters do not belong to any place, any time, any love, they are marked as threshold people of lost origin, with internal borders and divisions, unable to take root, a configuration of absences, with the present in abeyance. However, the spaces between belonging and not belonging can be positively inhabited—as Marion says in *Wings of Desire*: " I have no roots, no history, no country, and I like it that way. I'm here, I'm free. I can imagine everything; everything is possible . . . I only have to raise my eyes and once again I become the world." Finding/founding the present is one of the principal concerns of these films.

Kristeva argues that *meeting* balances wandering; it is a crossroads of two othernesses which owes its success to its provisional and temporary nature. The recent films are structured around such meetings: between angel and former angel, angel and human, Claire and the bank robber, Claire and Sam, European and Australian Aboriginal, angel and child, angel and corrupt businessman. These are often brief or transitory, moments of mutual recognition, the possibility or not of *being another*, which is the source of the ethical. In a world reduced, in Wenders's terms, to trading in images, cynicism and stock market deals, the issue of *strangers* comes up for the contemporary world which, having gone through the spirit of religion and other totalizing regimes of truth, once again encounters an ethical concern—one of the principal challenges of a secularised world. Kristeva contends (and I see similarities with Wenders) that we are, for the first time in history, confronted with the following situation: we must live with different people while relying on our personal moral codes, without the assistance of a set of codes that would include our particularities while transcending them (she is referring to those grand narratives which postmodernism has described).

Wenders is concerned with a similar condition, a paradoxical international community at the intersection of estrangement and familiarity. It is incomplete, fragmentary, fluid, and reterritorializing on almost anything—memory, fetish, icon or dream—that will restore an equivalent of territory, valid as home. Wenders says: "Identity means not having to have a home. Awareness, for me, has something to do with not being at home," echoing Adorno's comment, "it is part of morality not be at home in one's home." The films are preoccupied with a place that is neither "here" nor "there", with an identity that is both self and other, and a time that is then, now and, possibly, tomorrow. As new nationalisms confront existing international power blocs (Tony Baker in *Faraway* is German-American), is another form of post-nationalist, cross-cultural globalism possible? The extensive use of world music (ethnic, classical and rock) in each film opens up the possibilities of a newly accessible and popular form of cross-generic mutuality: a cultural dialogue. Reterritorialization is not simply a matter of place (the mystified ideological root of nationalism) but, in the first instance, a question of personal and *local* resource: of beginning again (a theme in all three films) which may well involve the severing of old ties and the making of sacrifices, but is also the motive of creativity.

The figure of Cassiel in *Wings of Desire* (1987) asks himself, "Are there any borders left?" and answers: "More than ever. Each street has its borderline." This was the Berlin of the mid-1980s. Changes since 1989 have refocused attention on the displaced person, the migrant and the stranger; people dispossessed of, and separated from, their identity and their history. This experience has to be seen in the context of a new global economy, criss-crossed by complex, overlapping and disjunctive national flows. This has led, in some instances, to the deconstruction of existing geopolitical boundaries, to internal crises of coherence and stability, and to the construction of new social spaces, at once globalized and local, predicated upon "migrant" identity—a fluid becoming in which there is the possibility of developing citizens of a borderless world in which national boundaries are anomalous (of course, there is the contrary experience—in Eastern Europe—of more borders than ever). In the realm of the cultural, a number of recent films by Wim Wenders are of critical importance for understanding this process.

The films made by Wenders in the period 1987-1994 are dominated by the following themes: memory, division, homelessness as home, urban and global spatiality, the presence of the stranger, loss and reconciliation. None of these themes figures in a singular or unproblematic way as the films explore how fragmentation, rupture and discontinuity can be transformed from crises of displacement to occasions for possibility and renewal: a fluid becoming based on "migrant" identity. In each film, characters seek to position themselves by choosing primary identities—often marginal or equivocal—which are capable of being articulated with flexible ways of being, of a radical openness. Reconciliation is never a matter of simple compromise, goodwill or cosy liberalism because it is always accompanied by potential risk, sacrifice, and conflicted interpretation. The key to all of this is vulnerability. The circumstances, the contexts of reconciliation are as crucial as the process itself.

In each of the films Wenders works with a fragmenting, dislocating and decentering mode of construction which is spliced with the critical and deliberative use of formulaic generic tropes from the popular realist thriller. In *Until the End of the World* (1991) and *Faraway, So Close!* (1993) there is a stylised and multi-layered hyper-plotting which both underpins the "quest" trajectory and subjects it to pastiche. The use of Peter Falk as a Columbo-like figure and as "himself" in the latter film and in *Wings of Desire* emphasises and plays with this. Neither popular nor canonical genre is subverted in the process as both co-exist in a dialogical relationship which confirms the stylised conventionality of each.

Wings of Desire is shot primarily in West Berlin (permission to film in the East was initially granted, but ultimately refused) but is constantly with, and up against, the Wall in a number of senses. *Faraway, So Close!* is located mainly in East Berlin and opens with a number of panning, aerial shots establishing through spectacle the terrain of the politically "unknown". It is informed throughout by post-1989 Europe, including a cameo appearance by Mikhail Gorbachev who—according to the preview programme notes—by introducing the concepts of *glasnost* and *perestroika* into international vocabulary, is credited with laying the groundwork for the opening up of the Eastern Bloc countries and the dismantling of the Berlin Wall. Gorbachev says of his collaboration with Wenders, "I think Wim Wenders and I knew each other without ever having met before. Chance brought us together. I got involved in the idea of the film, I liked the philosophy of it and gave my agreement" (quoted in the preview programme notes). The film is a sequel, in some ways, to *Wings of Desire*.

Until the End of the World, originally conceived as a science fiction film by Wenders in 1977, is set in 1999 and is less specifically related to post-1989 Europe, but concerned with aspects of the new global systems such as "time-space distantiation" and "space-time compression". What is left of the science fiction, apart from the high definition computer imaging, operates often at the level of pastiche (some of the technology has Bond-like features). Categories of globalisation focus on "the constant separation and dislocation of space by time" (Howarth, 1993: 52) which results in, what Giddens calls, "disembedding"—the continuous abstraction of social relations from the local and their recomposition in global contexts, like a sampling and re-mix process in music. I shall discuss later what happens to the global contexts in the film (Paris, Lisbon, Berlin, Tokyo, Beijing, Moscow, Venice, San Francisco—metropolitan "depthless" spaces) and the ways in which the local—the writer, the Aboriginal culture, the herbs in the garden in Japan—is recomposed as a site of reconciliation and potentiality.

Time, space and history/memory are problematised in all three films and in *Wings of Desire* and *Faraway, So Close!* are tied in with the role of the angels and their relation to the earth. Linked to this is the theme of the "stranger" who is always faraway and so close. I shall be drawing extensively on Georg Simmel"s 1908 essay "The Stranger" (Simmel, 1950) for much of this discussion.

The essay begins, "If wandering is the liberation from every given point in space, and thus the conceptional opposite to fixation at such a point, the sociological form of the 'stranger' presents the unity, as it were, of these two characteristics" (Simmel, 1950: 402). Simmel represents the stranger as the potential wanderer, "the person who comes today and stays tomorrow." In Wenders they include the angels Cassiel, Damiel and Peter Falk in *Wings of Desire* and *Faraway, So Close!*; Marion in *Wings of Desire*, and Claire and Sam (and arguably, from a Eurocultural perspective, the Aboriginal people) in *Until the End of the World*. Their position is determined (or undetermined) by the fact that they have not belonged to a location from the beginning (except for the Aboriginals who have been made strangers by an alien power), and they import qualities into it which cannot stem from the location itself. In a sense children (or more properly childhood) are always in this condition. The strangers combine nearness and remoteness, both outside the "group" and its mores and confronting it. They are metaphorical "traders", sources of expansion and new moral/cultural territories. The sedentary is defined by the border; the nomadic by border crossing.

Simmel points to the classical example of the stranger as supernumerary in the history of European Jews—restricted to intermediary trade, often to pure finance, and figures of mobility. Deprived in the figurative sense of a life-substance which is fixed, the Jew as "extra" is focused upon in *Wings of Desire* particularly, where original footage of Nazi Germany is imbricated with a modern, American filming of the period. Cassiel says of the film in rehearsal: "They could be the real thing, they look it" (although Wenders works always at, and across, the borders of the "real" and the "look like"). At one point a line from the film is spoken: "You're not natives, you're all refugees," reaffirming the idea of the Jew as stranger, but also linking with the other "wanderers" in modern Germany—the guestworkers and other nonindigenous peoples (itself a problematic term) subjected to racism. At another point—shown momentarily in colour (most of the film is shot in black and white, from the angels' perspective)—Cassiel sits next to an isolated Muslim woman in a laundromat. The woman vacuuming in the Berlin Library is also a Muslim. The Jew in Europe was historically confined to a single identity—pure finance; the non-German today to an identity confined to labour.

Peter Falk has come to Berlin to take part in an American film set in the Nazi period. He is a fallen angel, of German-Jewish descent. While he waits for his scenes he sketches people on the lot, wondering whether one of his subjects is Jewish (unlikely, given the context, but "looks like"; we remember that the uncertain Aryan/Jewish border had to be established by the wearing of the yellow star). He also says, "These people are extras —extra people. Extras are so patient—they just sit." "Extras—the easy ones [to draw] are extras, extra humans." The film term "extra" reminds us of Simmel's phrase "supernumerary" and that on the lot are "extras" playing the passive, victimised extra human, "extra" people—the Jewish people who synthesised nearness and distance, the feared objectivity of the stranger. The presence of the American film within the film enables Wenders to raise ethical questions about the aestheticisation of fascism, a cultural form of forgetting in which images usurp all other responses. Adorno's comments about the possibility, or otherwise, of poetry after Auschwitz come to mind here.

The angels in both *Wings of Desire* and *Faraway, So Close!* are also characterised as strangers, near in space (although invisible, except to the audience) but distant because they are out of time, only able to see monochromatically. Free, in a sense, and objective in terms of their perception, the angels understand and evaluate from a bird's eye view, yet their aerial perspective leaves them suspended and anachronistic, incapable of relationships or of translating their "vision" into action (Cassiel is unable to prevent the young man"s suicide on the East/West border in *Wings of Desire*; in *Faraway, So Close!* he gives up his life as an angel and becomes human when he catches the child, Raissa, when she falls ten stories from her balcony). The angels have only an abstract/theoretical relation with the human; they are privileged in their spatial, panning overview of history and event, but in Rilke's words: "And we, spectators always, everywhere, /looking at, never out of, everything!" (quoted in Wenders, 1991: 73)—denizens of the sky over Berlin (the German title of the film is *Der Himmel uber Berlin*).

Wenders chose Berlin to film in, as he felt that "the (hi)story that elsewhere in the country is suppressed or denied is physically and emotionally present here" (Wenders, 1991: 74). At the time this was written, the sky was seen as the only thing that united the two cities, and the angels represented a potential unity—seeing and knowing the past and present, of 1945 and 1986—but only able to shape a common future if they became human and entered time, uncertainty and the city, bringing a spiritual presence to this "ONE story about DIVISION" (Wenders, 1991: 76). In this film Damiel chooses to come to earth and, unsurprisingly, lands close to the Wall. In so doing, 1945 (the time when the angels came to Berlin) manifests itself in 1986 and, towards the end, 1986 manifests itself in 1945 with the setting of Damiel and Marion's love in the Hotel Esplanade, decadent and iconically fascist. In this film, the 1945-1986/1986-1945 dialectic is unresolved and (given the Wall) unresolvable.

The division in the film is a constant motif, with people seen in isolated shots and locations, alone and self-communing in episodic interior monologues (accessible only to the angels) a polyphony of undirected thoughts and voices—strangers even in their own city. The angels look down, but can do no more than look, assemble, testify, preserve in the manner of the objective intellectual. Their base is the Berlin Public Library—a place of classification and the repository of abstract knowledge, the cognitive but not the affective. Only children look up, from behind their parents.

The child, the angel and the storyteller/filmmaker (Homer, both angel and human, is as old as cinema itself) are all potentially healers of division, bringers of reconciliation because, for different reasons, they bear traces of spirituality; but they are all thrust to the edges of the world, or beyond. At the beginning of the film, Damiel is copying out a poem about childhood which refers to questions about identity, location, aesthesis and mortality; questions which originate from ideas (memories, perhaps) of unity and synthesis, but with an awareness of division, of nearness and of distance; the idea of child as "stranger", the potential wanderer.

In the library there is a reference to the fact that, in 1921, Walter Benjamin bought Paul Klee's *Angelus Novus* water-colour. In the Klee painting an angel is shown looking as though he is about to move away from something he is fixedly contemplating. Benjamin says: "This is how one pictures the angel of history. His face is turned toward the past. Where we perceive a chain of events, he sees one single catastrophe which keeps piling wreckage upon wreckage and hurls it in front of his feet. The angel would like to stay, awaken the dead, and make whole what has been smashed" (Benjamin, 1973: 259). Wenders's angels, turned toward the past (1945), see the single catastrophe of Nazism and are propelled into the future to "awaken the dead" and "make whole". Their dilemma is that the strategy involves mortality: the "storm of progress" and the condition of time, as time is the condition of narrative, with the angels occupying the visual space of spectacle.

This links with the storyteller, Homer, first encountered in the library, tracing the development of story from orality to the scriptural—"With time, those who listened to me became my readers—they no longer sit in a circle"; "They sit apart now, one knows nothing about the other." Another layer of estrangement is added to the text, compounded later when Homer is seen reading a book of war-time photographs. This scene is based in the library and intercut with Berlin 1945 footage, and Homer, stranded in the fissures and junctures of history, says: "No more sweeping over the centuries, moving back and forth through the past—Now I can only think day by day—My heroes are no longer warriors and kings." Nazism, and its aftermath, has foreclosed the possibility of epic, reduced narrative to the endlessly repeated quotidian. Over the images of corpses, Homer laments his inability to create an epic of peace: "what is it that makes its inspiration so unendurable?"

He says that if he gives up, mankind will lose its storyteller, and "once mankind has lost its storyteller it will have lost its childhood." Childhood, the storyteller, the angel and cinema itself, perhaps, are all the realm of the stranger: a very positive relation, a specific form of interaction because it is both faraway and so close. Inside yet outside, the "trader" (a figure of exchange and creativity) as stranger is the source and resource of mobility. In the film, however, strangers remain simply as unrealised, partial and fragmented potential, each with a different form of homesickness—the urge to be at home everywhere— all in a condition close to that described by Adorno in *Minima Moralia*: "For a man who no longer has a homeland, writing becomes a place to live"; but at the end of the section he writes: "In the end, the writer is not even allowed to live in his writing" (Adorno, 1974: 87). This, as Wenders sees it, is the condition of divided Berlin in 1986; no convenient narrative offers itself to "write" the history of the postwar city from the textualisation of fragmented images. Representation is, like the film itself, continuously interrupted and flawed, on the threshold of "no man's land," a borderline configuration no longer able to synthesise. Homer sums it up: "I won't give up as long as I haven't found the Potsdamer Platz," now an empty space of ruins, once filled with the activity of shops and tramways.

It is only when the angels achieve, what Derek Gregory calls, "corporeality of vision" and reach out from one body to another in "a spirit of humility, understanding, and care" (Gregory, 1994: 416), beyond individualism and corporatism, in *Faraway, So Close!* (as do the Mbantua elders in *Until the End of the World*, healing the body with the body) that space/time conjoin in a possible place for "writing" (in all senses of creativity).

Cassiel, sitting in the back of an old period car heading for the film lot asks: "Are there any borders left? More than ever! Each street has its border line. . . . The Germans are divided into as many states as there are individuals. . . .Each carries his own space with him and demands a toll from anyone who wants to enter, but to enter the interior of a state one must have a password." What the film is producing is a condition of late modernity: the ultimate logic of an individualist creed —being for yourself, *egological*.

Film, storyteller and angel all seek this password into an interior state, not in order to conquer and govern, but to liberate and heal, to reconcile. In this film, despite its ending (with its two principal characters self-absorbed, screened off and framed in isolation), this does not really ever happen.

In *Wings of Desire*, it is the angel Damiel who decides, "I want to transmute what my timeless downward gaze has taught me. I stood outside long enough. . . .I've been absent long enough. . . .I've been too long out of the world. . . .Let me enter the history of the world. . . if only to hold an apple." There are shots of Damiel only being able to grasp (literally) the idea of a thing, not the thing itself. Damiel's focus in the film is on the circus, in particular on Marion the French trapeze artist. The circus is a space of childhood, of strangers and of "near angels"—insider/outsiders. Apart from Marion's strangeness of origin, her attraction is her "flying"; she is likened by her companions to an angel, a dove and a lark. The film's first use of momentary colour features her shift from sitting to a position suspended from the trapeze—her unfixity, her mobility in space and her potential wandering place her close to Damiel as an object of beauty and love.

The circus closes as it cannot afford the rent or electricity. The bailiff appears and another space of childhood is foreclosed. Marion is revealed as ill at ease, melancholy, empty, fearful, sad and inadequate: "That's what makes me clumsy, the absence of pleasure." She says: "Here I am a foreigner, yet it's all so familiar," and, echoing one of the primary themes of the film, "Anyway, I can't get lost, you always end up at the Wall." There's another fractional shift to colour (this is the fragmentary glance of Damiel, still an angel at this stage) when she speaks of a desire to love, "a need to love," and Damiel, voyeur-like, watches her nakedness.

For Damiel, the circus—a space of children, creativity and performance—is analogous to the poem of childhood he transcribes: "When the child was a child . . . he had a precise picture of Paradise, now he can only make a guess." What is being referred to is the precognitive, the moment prior to thought. This is not simply a romantic lament, an idyll of lost childhood, but a record of time, change, radical openness and potentiality prior to the hegemony of the instrumental over the aesthetic, of time over space, of narrowing. The circus restores that space in the form of its ring, it stress on the body in motion, and its carnivalesque domain of strangers. Peter Falk also shows Damiel the value of being on earth: "I'm a friend . . . companero" —finally persuading him to enter through the "passes, the gates, and the crevices" of time.

Marion, alone at a concert, dancing to post-punk rock music says "I have a story . . . and I'll go on having one." It is this story, as well as Marion herself that Damiel seeks—to join a temporal narrativity. As a child (in a flashback sequence) Marion dreams the love of an angel. In

one of the most extended sequences of the film (in colour) after Damiel
has fallen to earth and found Marion, the film shifts from its fissure,
breaks and past-referencing discontinuities to a scene of reconciliation:
a romantic ending, with the couple framed in equal status shot, sharing
the space of the Hotel Esplanade. It is a moment of sustained decision
between strangers: organic, near and distant.

At one point, Marion celebrates the objectivity and freedom of the
stranger: " I have no roots, no history, no country, and I like it that way.
I'm here, I'm free. I can imagine everything. Everything is possible."
However, she, and they, are in Berlin: a place of roots, history and
country almost irreversibly corrupted by a time embodied in the very
hotel in which they meet—a rendezvous for the Nazi elite. It is this
spatial/cultural   reference   which   conditions,   undercuts   and
problematises the whole of this love sequence. As strangers they are
unaware of its symbolic specificity—an aporia (an irresolvable
moment) in which they participate, but of which they are not a part.

Marion sings of empowerment and possibility; of the accidental,
contingent and coincidental; above all, of choice. Both Marion and
Damiel opt emphatically for the present: "We incarnate something. . . .
we are sitting in the place of the people and the whole place is full of
people who are dreaming the same dream." The scene is self-
consciously representative, playing out a highly stylised and ritualised
"beginning again", a new Eden/Genesis myth, folding back time and
reentering the space of paradise: "There's no greater story than ours . . .
a man and a woman. It will be a story of giants, invisible but
transferable . . . a story of new ancestors."

The scene is archetypal—the picture of necessity, of everyone's
future. Yet, although Marion's name bears Mary who redeemed Eve, in
this new *origination*, she already wears the scarlet dress of the Whore
of Babylon, and in the close-ups which are filmed from Damiel's point
of view, as her face fills the screen we are aware of another archetype:
pale, blue-eyed, blonde—the ritualised/iconicised face of the Aryan
woman, speaking in an emphatically enunciated German in contrast
with her usual French. Marion is transformed, overdetermined by the
time and space of her "re-incarnation". It is a deeply contradictory,
potentially flawed moment, a moment of desire—"No mortal child was
begot but an immortal shared image"—and of genesis/apocalypse.
Damiel says, "She came to take me home and I found my home; she
made me a human being." They re-enact the entry of Adam and Eve
into time and mortality— home is a conflicted/ambiguous space—both
earth and West Berlin, a divided place, unreconciled, and filled with the

past. The question Wenders poses (in *The Logic of Images*) —"how to live? —will, as the credits suggest, have "to be continued."

The inflated, operatic language brings the scene close to comedy, but it also suggests that, although Damiel has landed in 1986, perhaps— culturally and psychologically—he has not managed to go beyond 1945. In *The Logic of Images* Wenders says, "The angels have been in Berlin since the end of the war, condemned to remain there" (Wenders, 1991: 79). Metaphorically, the rundown period hotel, the theatrical aesthetics and erotic discourse, and the exclusive couple framing suggest that the fascist "moment" remains untranscended. This sense is reinforced by the next scene in which Damiel assists Marion in her trapeze-rope routines, indicating the need for ascent, an aspiration which is based upon future action, not present rhetoric. Their love needs grounding in the complex and ongoing, time-based transience of the quotidian; it lacks human shape, corporeality of vision and the body of mortality.

The film does not end with the "assumption" of Marion and Damiel but, significantly, with Homer—in his empty spaces still—saying, "Name me the men, women and children who will look for me . . . me, their storyteller, their spokesman. For they need me more than anything in the world. We have embarked." The empty space of Damiel and Marion will have to be contextualized, made into a story which is not just their own.

Estrangement is an internal condition and is explored in the journey across space and time of *Until the End of the World*, a film of wandering and fixation, of homelessness and home, of ambivalence and difference—in a word, Derrida's word, *undecidability*. It is a multi-lingual and transnational film (with the cooperation of producers and art directors from seven countries) which features the stranger as novelist, rewriting the story of the group and enabling each figure to confront an absence within his or her habitual consciousness. For the Europeans and the Americans, that absence is also represented by the healing presence of the Mbantua Aboriginal peoples, the meeting between them producing a temporary mutuality and the opening up of a potential space, a crossing of a borderline: it is a meeting of two *othernesses*. The Aboriginals are physically proximate, but spiritually "elsewhere."

In *Faraway, So Close!* Damiel and Marion are featured with their daughter, Doria, in a series of minor, domestic-orientated roles—banal in comparison with the Lawrentian grandeur of *Wings of Desire*. Damiel is an Italian pizza maker with his own firm Casa dell Angelo, and Marion is still a trapeze artist. Their main function is to support

Cassiel when he becomes human; they have graduated to living for others. In retrospect, it is probably the Hotel Esplanade scenes which are banal, with Damiel and Marion now focused upon questions that Wenders is asking in each of his recent films: How to live, and what to live for? He argues that films avoid this questioning more and more and try by all means to escape from answering it. Cinema, he claims, has increasingly escaped what he calls "true cinema," and instead roots itself more and more in film, rather than in life. These three films all seek to go beyond aesthetic discourse as an end in itself.

The last comment is important because critical approaches to Wenders (for example, Robert Phillip Kolker and Peter Beicken, *The Films of Wim Wenders: Cinema as Vision and Desire*) often stress the knowing intertextuality and extensive cultural quotation. However, arguably, this is as much pastiche and as formulaic as is his use of popular genres to undercut a monological narrative. Like the stranger, the narrative cannot be singular and complete in terms of its own aesthetic; it has to sustain an always negotiable relationship with its other referent—a world constituted *otherwise*.

In a sense, Damiel's dream of arrival is predicated upon desire, and Cassiel's upon the ethical: how to bring his spiritual and ideal remoteness into line with a people seemingly absorbed and overwhelmed by the world. Cassiel says to his fellow angel Raphaela: "People haven't conquered the world, the world has conquered them . . . they seem to flee from each other." Apart from children (as seen in *Wings of Desire* also) no one looks up or beyond. The angels are the messengers who bring "closeness for those who are distant," harbingers of love and harmony (not as "givens" but as processes to be worked on and through) rather than blood and steel. The angel, like the stranger, has no originary point of return once committed to "being for others"; he is homeless, diasporic, living *now*, aware that there is nothing beyond the human. However, he also finds himself, in Schutz's terms, "a border case outside the territory covered by the scheme of orientation current within the group" and confined by liminality (Schutz, 1964: 99).

Lacking a strategy for orientation, Cassiel seeks to centre himself, to relocate himself in a Berlin which he finds intimidating. Literally homeless, released from gaol, at his lowest point he is rescued by a German-American businessman, Tony Baker. This moment marks both the onset of Cassiel's ethical dilemma and the film's entry into a thriller mode because Baker is a black market arms salesman, trading former East German weapons in exchange for pornographic and violent videos.

Wenders says (in the preview notes) "INSTRUMENTS of violence are traded for IMAGES of violence". Baker is also anxious to be reunited with his sister Hanna. They were separated in 1945 when Baker and his father left for the US, and his mother and sister were left in the care of Konrad, a chauffeur in Nazi Germany. Konrad becomes Cassiel's closest friend and "ethical" companion.

We see the pervasive intervention of markets into hitherto unpenetrated or resistant spaces. Cassiel becomes involved in the market, a space characterised by instruments of violence being traded for images of violence. The mock-thriller aspect of the film (partly subject to pastiche and cliché—aspects of humour disliked by many Wenders enthusiasts) summarises many of the principal features of a situation in which the self-interested market reduces everything to itself and its values: risk, competition, violence, surplus value and, ultimately of course, the struggle for monopoly. We see an image-soaked, derelict culture driven by *money*. Nazi imagery (a reel of film from a Nazi propaganda unit is used symbolically) is seen as continuous with the power of the market in some ways as the moral-political order (Baker is not by chance a German-American) is seen to have relinquished any ethical foundation.

The problem for Cassiel is how to respond and how to intervene— how to move from idea to action, to show that all humans have the capacity to look up and beyond, but that most, except for children and others not taken seriously, have lost the power. He rehearses, in synoptic fashion, three stages of growth: the isolated being for itself in closed space, the forming of a relationship with one other (the chauffeur, Konrad) and, eventually, the broader "political" engagement in a collective action with a number of marginal figures whose survival depends upon a mutuality of skills —the circus people.

First of all, Cassiel has to enter time, mortality and interhuman relationships (he does this at a moment when a vulnerable "other" calls to him and he enters the realm of ethical responsibility). For Wenders, thinking in this *ethical* perspective is a precondition of a new moral-political order. Time, then, fashions Cassiel's relationship with the other. Now he has to live from one moment to another without ever being able, like an angel, to retrieve it, to catch up with, or coincide with, it. He has sacrificed simultaneity for sequence (compare the way in which the thriller works with a time-based plot) even though he is tempted by Time itself (Dafoe) to trade in his human status and return to the angelic. No longer can Cassiel listen in to the thoughts of any other person; he has to learn human resources: other humans are now beyond him, irreducibly *other*. Cassiel discovers sociality, reciprocity and collective ethical action. He finds out that relationships with others are better as difference than as sameness.

In one of the climactic scenes of the film, in a remarkable display of alternative forms of power, he joins in the possibility of going beyond market values to something which challenges these —a disruption of our simply being in the world for ourselves as passive consumers that opens us up to the vulnerable other who must have primacy. This unsettles the commonsensical and so-called political realism of our everyday practices. Compared with market freedom—image and consumer dominated—ethical freedom is, what has been called by Levinas, "a difficult liberty." It was always much easier for Wenders to work with division, negativity and disillusion—with, that is, the current which is both dependent upon and frustrated by the limits of a materialist ideology.

The film interleaves (but does not elide) the Nazi and East German experience, the affective realm and the corrupt world of business. Baker's empire is challenged by Patzke, who is outwitted by Cassiel when he threatens Baker's life (by means of the Hollywood Mafia cliché of setting his legs in concrete).

In *Faraway, So Close!* Wenders extends the conception of angels from that in *Wings of Desire*. He introduces a figure, Emit Flesti, with the double capacity of entering both the angelic and earthly worlds. As his name (Time itself) suggests he is a timekeeper, and conspires to end Cassiel's human experience, taking on a sinister role and conflicting with Raphaela over Cassiel's fate in the human world. Cassiel, punningly, assumes identity as Karl Engel (in a way, the film's comedic form is closest to the structures of *The Tempest*, another "thriller").

Having been jailed, destitute and homeless, Cassiel's synoptic, and exemplary, experience of contemporary post-Cold War Europe leads him to an ethical action which involves damaging the videos (many of them featuring Nazi memorabilia), seizing the weapons and removing them to safety by boat. At the same time, Hanna and Raissa's links to Baker make them vulnerable to attack from Patzke, and Cassiel arranges for Konrad to "complete" the flight of 1945 by taking them to the docks to escape by the same boat.

What Cassiel is doing is participating in the epic of peace referred to by Homer in *Wings of Desire*, by destroying the violence and its seeds. The year 1945 as the definitive symbolic moment of violence (the weapons and videos are stored in old Nazi vaults, and Baker's father worked in the Nazi propaganda film unit; the complicity of film is a sub-theme of the text) is replayed constantly through icon, flashback and footage. It is also faraway, so close: a continuing "absent" presence. Emit Flesti kills the detective, Phillip Winter, who may have been able to unravel the mystery of Tony Baker, the link with Hanna, Raissa, Konrad and the Nazi period, thus suppressing the continuity between past and present which needs the stranger's perspective.

In order to carry out the complex task of dismantling Baker's illegal (immoral) empire, Cassiel calls upon the help and unusual skills of Marion's circus people. Patzke discovers what is happening, kidnaps Tony Baker and takes the whole boat hostage. Aided by circus apparatus, Cassiel decides upon an ethical action—being for others—which puts at risk his own humanity. Becoming an "angel" again, he flies on the trapeze and rescues Hanna's daughter and Baker's niece, Raissa. He succeeds, but in doing so is shot dead, although his intervention has enabled Patzke to be overcome and Baker, Hanna and Raissa to be reconciled. Cassiel rejoins Raphaela as an angel.

Damiel's "dream of arrival" in *Wings of Desire*—idealised, theoretical, aesthetic—is completed by Cassiel's journey through alienation, despair and liminality to an orientation in action, a moral space in which proximity and distance are synthesised. Reconciliation is also revelation—knowledge picks up from the point of breach, disruption and ambivalence. Classification, norms and habitual behaviour have been threatened/challenged by the stranger's actions. Action is, of course, the realm and medium of the thriller, but Wenders uses a mock-thriller device, with both "detectives" (Winter and Cassiel) dead, and the restored "moral universe" not a metaphysical/ transcendental *given*, but a space of possibility dependent upon future human action making sense of reconciliation: the ethical transaction itself. Future action—"how we live?"—will determine whether or not Cassiel's whole intervention will be merely an episode incapable of making a permanent mark.

In *Faraway, So Close!* Cassiel is the stranger as trader—realising the time is out of balance because of the primacy of money—carrying out a reverse trade in which both the objects of exchange are destroyed. Ethical transactions, communal togetherness are inimical to the institutions of modern society, pre-or post-Cold War.

Bauman, in *Postmodern Ethics*, talks about the objects of cognitive spacing as being "the others we live *with*. The objects of moral spacing are the others we live *for*" (Bauman, 1993: 165). At the end of *Wings of Desire*, Damiel and Marion are living in an aesthetically spaced world, a social space which depends upon mobility, flight, and intensity. The aesthetic is premised upon the novel and the surprising, the mysterious and the sublime (Damiel and Marion do not "know" each other). Bauman claims that "aesthetic spacing cannot—must not—hold objects in place"; it is "totally consumed in the process of spacing" (Bauman, 1993: 180), as has been demonstrated above. In *Faraway, So Close!* we see Damiel and Marion in moral space created around affection, responsibility and familiarity. They accept the limits and constraints, but coinhabit both a moral and an aesthetic space—with the circus and their child, a source of the sublime, the unknown and the recondite.

The cooperation of Cassiel and the circus people—a complex network of mutuality—in dismantling Baker's business marks the shift of Cassiel from being merely human to becoming a moral agent. It is not, however, without ambivalence or risk, as the consequences of his act are beyond his control. With Patzke overpowered, how might Baker manipulate a situation in which his family reconciliation coincides with the presence of the missing weapons? It is an unanswerable question, but it shows the undecidability, the endemically ambivalent nature of Wenders's work; it is unresolved, beyond closure, conditional and without guarantee.

Post-Cold War Europe is new and unprecedented. In moving through the space other people live in, Cassiel seeks to mark his journey, to create a memory of himself not through heroism, monument or wealth but through the agency/example of peaceful coexistence. It is harder to find a cinematic discourse of possibility, of renewal, of ethical answerability as opposed to one of narcissism and estrangement. Nor do I think Wenders necessarily achieves this with *Faraway, So Close!* but that may be the point: he is working within the tradition of the political fable, of the allegorical. Because of deep end-of-century cynicism, the ethical relation always seems unrealistic and utopian (literally "out of place") in our everyday world. We are so absorbed by western secular meanings, or complicit western religious forms, that the possibility of an ethical and collective movement seems beyond our imagination (in the sense that we have no image vocabularies for it). This is Wenders's dilemma: imagining a world beyond a self-interest which is itself attached to property, and taking over what is other than ourselves for ourselves—always entering the places of the other person wherever possible.

The film's "instability" of style and form echoes the ambivalence of the moral condition but, at least, creates a space in which "the possibility to act on the promptings of moral responsibility must be *salvaged*, or *recovered*, or *made anew*; against odds . . . the responsibility must exchange its now invalidated or forgotten priority for the superiority over technical-instrumental calculations" (Bauman, 1993: 185; emphasis in original). This attempt to restore forgotten priorities may explain why it took so long for *Faraway, So Close!* to find a British distributor, and why *Lisbon Story* (1994) was not released in the US for two years and not at all in the United Kingdom.

Technical-instrumental calculations—the medium of what Beck calls the "risk society"—form the backdrop to *Until the End of the World* (1991). It works with "technology-induced fragmentarity" which it uses as a formal, cinematic resource—an enabling narrative—and also places it critically along lines suggested by Bauman:

I propose that the technology-induced fragmentarity, which at one pole results in the concealment of the systemic nature of the human habitat, and on the other in the dissembly of the moral self, is a major . . . cause of what Ulrich Beck . . . dubbed *Risikogellschaft* (Risk Society). The problem-focused quest for efficiency, admittedly technology's most powerful and vaunted asset, rebounds in unco-ordinated maximisation drives. Even if each drive is effective in resolving the task at hand . . . the global result is the constantly increasing volume and intensity of systemic imbalances. The strategy that gained its laurels from its spectacular success in the construction of local orders, is itself a major factor of the fast growing global disorder. (Bauman, 1993: 199)

The title of the film has a spatial (the Antipodes) and temporal (nuclear catastrophe) reference. The principal figures in the text experience, what Simmel called, that *wandering* which is the liberation from every given point in space—the ceaseless journeying of the unbelonging. To his original science fiction project, Wenders adds a love story which becomes the axis of the plot.

Set in 1999, at the time of an Indian nuclear satellite accident—a symptom of systemic imbalance and global disorder—Claire Tourneur, bored, hedonistic, feeling betrayed by her lover Eugene, restless and seeking adventure (high on drugs, drink and partying), crashes her car, gains a large amount of stolen money by chance and, also by chance, meets Sam Farber who is travelling around the world on a risky mission for his scientist father. The mission is "for his father" in the sense also that the film explores the "abandonment" of the son by the indifferent, endlessly demanding father whose love seems remote or, at best, utterly conditional. This is contrasted with the mutuality and reciprocity of the Aboriginal peoples, with elders passing on the law to the younger people and with a son helping his father to Edith's funeral.

Mobility, drift, pleasure, the novel and the surprising—the substance of aesthetic spacing —dominate the film initially, as Sam, technical and instrumental, is followed around the world by Claire. Their relationship is founded on ambivalence, compounded by the presence of a private detective, Phillip Winter, who, chasing Sam, alternately colludes with and deludes Claire who is trying to track Sam. As with the other two films discussed, a thriller element is introduced, "driven" by Winter with his sophisticated electronic surveillance equipment and banal slogans.

In the film many borders are crossed and cities visited, but both border and city dissolve in an iconic/technological sameness—filled but empty spaces, signs of a borderless, continuous world but also of global disorder. These empty city spaces contrast with the "lunar" landscapes of the Australian desert. These landscapes are places which embody aeons of time and are only empty to the European eye; to the Aboriginal peoples the desert is filled with meaning. The distinction between European and Aboriginal is not so clear-cut, however, as one of the urban Aboriginals, Bert, accompanying the Europeans to the Mbantua area has to refind his "country." He is aided in the process by a one-armed European who teaches him to play the didjeridoo. There are other examples of this cross-over, the most spectacular being the extended jam session where Aboriginal and European musicians combine, share and exchange instruments and musical styles (Eugene, the writer, vamps on the piano), and create a new cross-cultural sound: the blooming of a global music, one of the purposes of the journeys throughout the film. Another example of this fusion is the Aboriginal figure of Peter who is compiling a Mbantua/English dictionary and also plays electric guitar. No one is standing still for the ethnographer's gaze.

Many of the cities visited are those that have assumed increasing importance as the new economic order globalizes—Tokyo, Los Angeles, Paris, London. These are, what Manuel Castells has called, "informational cities" (Castells, 1989), dehistoricised and culturally rootless. In this world, information flows through networks and across vast distances, and "the historical emergence of the space of flows. . . [supercedes] the meaning of the space of places" (quoted in LeGates and Stout, 1996: 451). Wenders in this film, like Castells in *The Informational City*, is seeking to reconcile the "new techno-economic paradigm" with "place-based social meaning". This is particularly apparent in the extended, five hour version of the film when the European/American inhabitants of the "space of flows" meet with the

Australian Aboriginals with their "place-based social meaning." As Castells writes, "at the cultural level local societies, territorially defined, must preserve their identities, and build upon their historical roots, regardless of their economic and functional dependence upon the space of flows" (LeGates and Stout, 1996: 451). The territorial definition of the Aboriginal peoples is not characterised by a sentimental retreat into some kind of pastoral utopia, but, as will be shown below, their grasp of the "new techno-economic paradigm" is articulated with a sense of the past and of cultural traditions deeply rooted in "country" and a place-based community. The Europeans/Americans, with one exception (Sam's mother, Edith), have isolated themselves from the local societies. The five-hour version (according to Wenders there was also an eleven-hour cut) places much more focus on the Aboriginal peoples, especially the children, and their role in the film is more developed and less gestural than in the commercially released 150-minute version.

The commercial cut, although abrupt in the editing and severely truncated, is fairly effective in rendering the "space of flows" through the rapid cutting sequences. This version also gives a strong sense of alienation and loss, but its emphases make it a "European" film, with the Australian sequences seeming more like an appendix. The five-hour version slows everything down—with longer takes, pauses and silences—and a greater sense of the passing of time and of space as location gives the film a more reflective quality.

Until the End of the World works with Lukacs's idea of "transcendental homelessness" (the realm of film itself) and the notion of homelessness as home, as well as against the sentimental German *heimat* film. Transience, displacement, fragmentation are both the condition of the world as evidenced by its cities and the experience of the principal characters, operating within a purposeful/purposeless dialectic. Time-space distantiation, "disembedding", and the logic of globalisation remind us, in Pierre Nora's terms, that "There are *lieux de memoire*, sites of memory because there are no longer *milieux de memoire*, real environments of memory" (Nora, 1989: 7). The technology makes possible a process of *virtual* globalization, the experience of everything in the terms of distantiated relations. The western characters move across undifferentiated locations dependent upon nothing but access to an advanced technological infrastructure. It is only in the Australian desert that differentiation is confronted. Politically and economically, the Aboriginal peoples have long been disarticulated from the organisations of power, but, as the film shows, culturally they have never finally submitted to their control. At the "end of the world." traces of cultural and social meaning are reconstructed and mobilised—especially through the medium of music shared cross-culturally—in the form of localised identities staked out against, and yet ultimately in articulation with, spatial logics and by means of symbolic action and communication codes which have value and currency beyond the local. As will be argued below, the film reconstructs the cultural meaning of locality but not in a romantic or Luddite sense, as technology is affirmed by placing it within a human scale.

Nora's phrase "sites of memory" links with Sam Farber's quest for images for his blind mother to see, recorded on a camera developed by his father, which takes pictures that blind people can see. The camera not only records what is seen, but also the response to what is seen—the visual and cognitive. Sam visits "sites" of memory in many continents, travelling to metropolitan spaces hollowed out as "real environments of memory." These cities contrast with the spatial and territorial landscapes of Central Australia, seemingly abandoned in the 1990s after severe drought but actually inhabited by Mbantua Aboriginal peoples—nomadic, physically proximate yet spiritually remote—estranged in their own land but through the "Dreaming" living in a real environment of a memory of origin.

Nazism is an informing presence in this film, as Edith and Henry (Sam's parents) met in Lisbon as teenagers in flight from fascism. In a sense always in flight, Henry's life takes refuge in technical-instrumental calculations; his experiments seek to colonise the unconscious, open up dreams. He is attempting to synthesise the cognitive, visual and the conceptual to produce "virtual reality" but in the process limits himself to cognitive space—intellectual constructs based upon the acquisition and distribution of scientific knowledge: indifference, impersonality and pure reason. Wanted by the U.S. Government, in dispute with him over intellectual property rights, he flees America and is finally tracked down by the CIA, returned to the States and dies.

His wife, Edith Eisner, lost her sight at age eight. An ethnographer, she came to work with the Mbantua women at the end of the 1950s, presumably working initially within a classical, scientific paradigm. However, contrary to Eurocentric myths, Aboriginal people are shown as having a capacity for high technology balanced with, *meeting* with, the sacred. As the ophthalmologist says, without them nothing would have been possible. They introduce Edith and Henry to new kinship forms such as skin-brother and skin-sister, and Sam has a skin-mother and a skin-father. The displaced, the rootless and the refugee find "home" with the nomadic, the "homeless" (one of the characters says "home is where you go when you run out of places"). In the place of the Dreaming—their "country"—their presence restores a past-present-future continuum out of the fragmentary. Each of the principal figures requires a distancing from home, to become a stranger in order to go beyond the apocalyptic —the end of the world —and think again in the future perfect tense: the time to come.

The Mbantua Cultural Centre might seem either a romantic or a "colonised" space, secondary to the Farber project, but when Henry proposes to use his camera " to suck out our dreams and look at them like television," the Aboriginal people all leave the Project as, at this juncture, they decide to subordinate technology to their idea of the sacred. In the terms argued earlier, this is *not* a romantic trope in the film, but an exodus into a moral space, albeit ambivalent: the salvaging and making anew referred to above.

After Edith experiences her "second seeing", despite her joy at the images of her relatives, she realises that the world she is looking at again—for the first time in more than fifty years—is not all right, as Henry claims (in his cave of science he sees only reflections/images) but a darker and uglier world. Shortly after her experience she dies— "I just let go," she says—telling Henry, "I have seen finally after all these years—this is our story, my darling—what a chase it has been, what a dance."

Edith's funeral ceremony is carried out according to the rites of the Mbantua people; Henry observes these traditions, but neglects those for mourning. Obsessed, Kurtz-like he pursues a new line of research: recording his own dreams. Sam and Claire are seduced into this new research, and the three of them become totally self-absorbed, addicted to their dreams, and drowning in nocturnal imagery. For Henry, the shapes of a new universe emerge, confounding Freud and Jung, in which he sees the human soul singing to itself, the god within us. Showing Claire an image of a human "dreamed" on the screen, he says " it needs nothing"; she replies, "it needs everything" (this is before her own addiction). In a womb-like rock space—the headquarters of the scientific project—they regress to a complete image-narcissism: presocial, separate, and utterly individualistic. Claire is rescued by her former lover, Eugene, the writer who has tracked her across the world. The batteries on her image machine run out, and, "caged", she suffers violent withdrawal symptoms.

The latter stages of the film are crucial in so far as they interrogate technological dependency. The satellite accident causes the computers, and all other electronic communications media, to crash, and this calls for a response using other resources—mechanical (the truck started by a crank handle), cultural, musical, moral, imaginative and social—to restore balance. In a film dominated by technology, with figures constantly crossing boundaries, the question arises, what happens now? The answer given by one of the characters is "that's for you to invent."

Invention and imagination come into play as means of creating an internal social space in which the stranger can form a relationship with society. His computer down, Eugene is forced to complete his novel (and, by analogy, the film we are watching) using pencil and paper and, eventually, an obsolete manual typewriter. He writes in a cave surrounded by some of the earliest instances of human communication: cave paintings. At one point, he says, " I believed in the magic, the healing power of words and of stories," and that there is "no cure for the disease of images" which Henry, Sam and Claire suffer from.

There are cures, there is healing, but the film does not have a neat resolution. The love of Sam and Claire is over; Eugene's love is revealed as, ultimately, disinterested and unconditional—he is capable of a nonproprietary being with others in a non-command relationship. Claire and he have no romantic future. Eugene grows into the position of Lukacs's "transcendental homelessness" and of Simmel's stranger as trader/writer simultaneously inside and outside, writing the story of their "dance around the planet." Wenders originally conceived the film as *The Odyssey* told from Penelope's (Claire's) point of view, with Eugene as the story's Homer, a writer documenting this story (Horton, 1997: 4). Eugene wrote so that nothing would be forgotten, especially as he had no way of knowing if the catastrophe they had experienced was local or global (it is both). The dance (we see glimpses of Mbantua dance from a distance), music (Gabon pygmy children singing enters creative dialogue with western forms in a nonhierarchical, positive globalisation)and Mbantua healing practices all combine, after the failure of technology, in, what Celan calls "the singable remains."

This all sounds romantic and reactionary, a critique taken up by Kolker and Beicken:

Until the End of the World is a film of uncertainty in which redemption is reaction. The figure who survives most intact is a cuckolded husband [Eugene], a writer who loses his computer files and re-creates his novel on an old-fashioned typewriter in the Australian outback. His wife [sic; Claire] flies around the earth in a satellite, scanning earth for ecological disasters. Modernity has been reduced, awkwardly, to the romantic, the adorable, and the politically banal, while visions of technology are condemned and the old ways of storytelling are celebrated in retrospect and, perhaps, in bad faith. The imagination seeks *Heimat* in a heap of images, old and new, masquerading as postmodernity. (Kolker and Beicken, 1993: 164)

This insistently binary approach fits their thesis, but not the film (no mention whatsoever is made of the Mbantua people in their analysis). It is not a question of Aboriginal healing as good (as part of his recovery, Sam sleeps between two Mbantua elders who take his dreams) and modern technology as bad, but a matter of use and "ownership." The satellite at the end is using the same technology as the Indian nuclear satellite (which threatens the end of the world), but for a radically different purpose. Eugene resorts to a typewriter in the absence of a word processor, not in place of it. At the end he is communicating with Claire on her birthday via video satellite—he does not send a home-made card! Claire had been a geologist—a "place-identity" science— therefore working for Greenspace seems logical enough. Whether it is politically banal to harness technology to monitor its ecological abuses is a moot point. It is not Eugene as such who survives most intact, but his *function* as maker, storyteller, agent of the healing power of words and of stories.

It is the capacity for imagination and invention, cultural *and* technological (it is the abuse of technology, its use as an instrument of power either by the U.S. government or Henry which is placed critically), which the film seeks to sustain, in a both-and dialogical relationship. There is no redemption as such; the world does not end— this time —but its continuance depends upon a number of possibilities, of creative spaces none of which is prescriptively filled. In fact, the resources laid out in the film need to be seen metaphorically, rather than simply empirically. The world of technologically created images has colonised and hegemonised ways of seeing, thinking and, above all, imagining. Wenders is not saying that writers and Aboriginal healers will save the world, but that their resources, functions and disinterestedly used powers can renew a radical openness and modes of possible collectivity, closed down by image-marketing and violence which have become the primary activities of technology as it has been hijacked by capitalist relations of production and exchange for cultural, and all other, forms of imperialism.

In the words of Ulrich Beck, "how one lives becomes the *biographical solution of systemic contradictions*":

the biography is increasingly removed from its direct spheres of contact and opened up across the boundaries of countries and experts for a *long-distance morality* which puts the individual in the position of potentially having to take a continual stand. At the same moment as he or she sinks into insignificance, he or she is elevated to the apparent throne of a world-shaper. (Beck, 1992: 137; italics in original)

World-shaping, I would argue, if this does not sound too pretentious, is the core of Wenders's project in these three films.

Chapter 5

Mutualities: The Search for a Lost Narrative

To simplify for a moment, it is possible to say that all Wim Wenders's films since the early 1980s have been concerned with what might be called *storying* —the search for narrative. With *Reverse Angle* and *The State of Things* (both 1982) he focused on what he perceived to be the specific threat to film images. This is why the framing of images, the relatively long takes and the use of deep space and depth of field are so prominent in *Paris, Texas*. The composition of the image is a matter of precision and careful definition. Unlike most Hollywood films, which are shot in an aspect ratio of 1.85:1, the film is shown in the widely used European wide-screen format of 1.75:1.

The specific threat to film images came, for Wenders, from the Hollywood media industry which, he argues, "reduced all images to the same level of artificiality and calculated effect." He saw this as part of a postmodern deterioration of images. At the same time, however, Wenders was also deeply influenced by certain aspects of American popular culture—rock music, automobiles and western movies; all of these feature in *Paris, Texas* but not simply as images/icons but in a contextualised fashion. Part of his oppositional strategy to Hollywood was an attempt to structure his films tightly around a central narrative which was not a feature of the road movies of the 1970s or even of *The American Friend*. The new emphasis is on deeply constructed, framed and focused narrative contexts which can contain images in a new web of meaning: "I want to find a narrative cinema that avidly and with self confidence establishes a connection between film art and life, and which no longer needs to reflect its own textuality in the narrative . . .A fresh start in film narrative that's my goal" (Cook and Gemünden, 1997: 77).

Not only was there a concern with narrative but also with ways of seeing. Wenders warned that the objective power of the camera to describe things in a vigilant manner so that they can appear in the proper light (the way "they are") is diminishing. At the end of *Reverse Angle*, somewhat apocalyptically, Wenders quotes the artist Cezanne: "Everything is about to disappear. You've got to hurry up, if you still want to see things." "I hope it's not too late," he comments (Cook and Gemünden, 1997: 44).

Oddly enough, in a colloquium on narrative techniques in Italy in 1982, Wenders said that he has always had nothing but problems with stories, and that his stories always start from images and the setting up of particular shots, *mise-en-scene*. So, in his practice, he saw an opposition between images and stories, as if they were working against each other. Images, he says, have always interested him more. His stories always begin with places, cities, landscapes or roads: a map is like a script for Wenders.

On the other hand, Wenders sees writers as people who seem to come up with stories because of the logical connections inherent in narration—every word tends to belong to a sentence, and sentences tend to belong to a coherent whole. Connectivity and sequence seem to be the primary characteristics of narrative. Conversely, Wenders sees that his images do not necessarily lead to something else; they stand on their own. For him, telling stories means forcing images into something.

Interestingly enough, many of Wenders's 1970s films were shot in chronological sequence, without any clear dramatic structure. *Paris, Texas* followed the more traditional method of nonchronological, piecemeal filming whereby production concerns determined the sequencing. In the original shooting script this sequencing timetable is quite clear. So, although the principal male character is disoriented, and disorientation is a key theme of the 1970s films, this film is very much structured. Sam Shephard's screenplay helps provide this forward movement, this sense of a very straight line.

Speaking in 1991, Wenders argued that cinema was going through a transition similar to the all-encompassing and revolutionary change from silent to sound film: "the age of photography, of the photographic image, and thus of cinema itself, is coming to an end and we are entering the era of the digital-electronic image" (Cook and Gemünden, 1997: 50). Ten years earlier he had seen television and video as "archenemies." Now he sees a new language of high-definition, electronically mastered images. He is also optimistic that Hollywood imperialism will not simply swamp "poor" little national film productions, but that there will be an increasing awareness of "European" cinema as a proud common language across a range of countries, and a European industry with its own institutions that can guarantee the survival of smaller national industries.

Lisbon Story (1994) revisits many of these themes and opens up again the image/story conflict in the context of a "new" Europe. The film was shown at Cannes in 1995, and its themes are clearly related to the origins of cinema and the centenary of film exhibition in the form of a comedy which plays with the silent-image/sound-image history of movies. Rudiger Vogler, who has appeared in seven other Wenders's films, repeats his Phillip Winter role and, responding to a postcard from his film-maker friend, Friedrich Monroe takes to the road en route to Lisbon. The setting in Portugal, the western edge of Europe facing in the direction of America, and the character of Friedrich, played by Patrick Bauchau, return us to Wenders's 1982 film, *The State of Things*, a polemic against the Hollywood image industry. Although the lead actor and the location are the same, the stance in the earlier film is now subject to critical scrutiny. Where *The State of Things* endorsed the European auteurist position and gave priority to images over narrative, the later film, as its title suggests, points to certain absurdities in Friedrich's over-dramatic claims for the "pure" image and resistance to new technologies. Both films explore the nature of creativity but the second production takes itself far less seriously.

On the road, Winter speculates on the ways in which Europe has become one place now with landscapes which all speak the same language, telling stories of an old continent in which the ghosts of history pass through its inhabitants. Portugal was the base for the first European seaborne empire and, in featuring its capital, the film in a sense is charting a return to a space in which Europe of the late twentieth century can reflect upon a nonimperial and unified continental identity and culture, mapping a different course. The narrating figure, Winter, tries to learn Portuguese but, interestingly, all the young children in the film speak English. Children, as always in Wenders, are harbingers of the future, bearers of clear vision, and the use of English in the film is not just for marketing reasons but is also there as a sign of a potentially shared identity. Although the film pays homage to the past and to the history of cinema, with its tributes to Vertov and Buster Keaton, it is also very much a film about the possibilities of a future cinema and a future Europe. Friedrich is attached umbilically to an old hand-cranking camera whereas the children, and Winter increasingly, are at home with the latest camera technologies. As is so often the case the case with Wenders's films, the children "are present as the film's own fantasy, the eyes the film would like to see with. A view of the world that isn't opinionated, a purely ontological gaze" (Wenders, 1997: 43). It is a romantic view but one that is not necessarily sentimentalising about the innocence of children as such, but about a particular way of looking, a gaze which is, in a sense, precognitive, anterior to thought.

Upon reaching Lisbon, Winter experiences a range of Keatonesque accidents and misfortunes, symptomatically breaking down at the border and being forced to take a lift with a horse and cart. This cart ride, together with a number of references to a disappearing past, is not simply an act of nostalgia but an attempt to open up a dialogue and a continuity between past and future, against Friedrich's refusal to acknowledge that the whole history of cinema has happened. As a reluctant and partial recognition of this, Friedrich had summoned Winter to Lisbon to help with the sound for the movie he is making of the city. Arriving at the city to find Friedrich has disappeared, Winter reverts to an earlier detective role and searches for his friend. This search becomes, simultaneously, the narrative and the form of the Lisbon story, an archival study both in sound engineering and the archaeology of the various layers of the city, bringing to light the stories that were hiding. The local children become guides and interpreters; it is they who decode the narrative of sound effects which Winter constructs. It is these sounds which are produced through studio mimicry and simulation, as well as by direct recording from the "real", which underline the *made*, mediated and arbitrary nature of film and give the lie to Friedrich's ideology of pure imagery.

At Friedrich's house, Winter discovers the group Madredeus who are producing the music for Friedrich's film, and he falls in love with Teresa, the vocalist, whose voice has echoes of a traditional folk acoustic articulated with a pop vernacular. Their romantic soundtrack (fado mixed with folk) is the complement to Winter's mix of ambient and artificial material. The film is very much about matching sound to image, and Madredeus provides an entry to the city and a way through it as Winter locates the originals of Friedrich's images and collects the effects for postdubbing edits in his improvised Foley studio. The moment when Winter ironically records the sound of Friedrich's absence marks the prelude to the recognition that the film-maker is locked away in the world of silence/silents, frozen in 1928, the year of Keaton's *The Cameraman* which the film invokes at several points. The sad-clown figure of Winter acts as a catalyst for Friedrich, making the completion of his film possible not only though the production of sound but also through his love for Teresa, so that, as he says, "you can make images in your heart on magic celluloid." As one of the Madredeus lyrics states, "the one who moves forward keeps his love, keeps his hopes." Friedrich leaves a note in his diary which comments on his having to read by candlelight, and cites an extract from the First Letter to Corinthians: "If I had not love, I am nothing." Since returning to Christianity, Wenders has used biblical texts in other films, but the love in *Lisbon Story* is also quite clearly of a secular/human nature. Love, images and seeing are, in many senses, at the centre of the Wenders's films of the 1990s.

Apart from Madredeus, whose music and lyrics help shape the film's aesthetic, Winter also discovers the writings of the Portuguese poet Pessao, left in his room by Friedrich. He traces the lines highlighted by Friedrich which all refer to ways of seeing: "in broad daylight even the sounds shine . . . I have wanted like sounds to live by things and not be theirs"; "I listen without looking and so see."

A cameo by the writer/director Manoel De Oliveira on film-making brings into focus a number of the themes of the film, particularly its stress on artists recreating and rethinking the world ("as if they were little gods") and the problematic nature of memory with its unbridgeable gap between past event and our imaging/imagining of it. The link with the illusion/invention, the mediated quality, of film itself is made explicit, and Friedrich's commitment to pure, uncontaminated imagery is placed in critical perspective.

When Winter finally tracks Friedrich down, he claims that he is no longer making the film which Winter has spent three weeks working on, and they meet in a derelict cinema. In the cinema, the whole history of film exhibition is reprised while Winter listens silently to Friedrich's hectoring fantasies about a pure aesthetic of the image. Friedich repeats some of Wenders's own 1980s positions about images no longer telling but selling stories and how he wanted to oppose the current drift by making films in black and white on an old "hand cranker", starting from scratch all over again and subverting the violence of the camera: "pointing a camera is like pointing a gun." The intervening hundred years of cinema history renders this totally illusory as he discovers that, as he cranked and cranked, the city gradually receded. He had reached the absurd point where he began to stockpile a vast library of unseen images on the basis that the uncontaminated image—shot with nobody looking through the lens—would blend with its object in perfect unison, thus erasing a century of moving-picture history. What he seeks to eliminate is the human from the aesthetic context. Winter guides

Friedrich to a realisation of the dead-end nature of this terminus vision, and, appropriately, the film ends with the two of them on a tram, starting out again, in Keaton fashion, to revisit and re-vision Lisbon: to story its images in *moving* pictures, a reference both to effect and affect.

It has to be said about both *Lisbon Story* and the feature film which followed it, *The End of Violence* (1997), that the ideas and issues they deal with are potentially of more significance than the cinematic narratives which are produced. Although in both films Wenders identifies a particular subject, or subjects, and allows that subject to define itself in the course of the film, the relatively incoherent and somewhat disjointed form of the films works against their effectiveness as studies in reconciliation, both cultural (in terms of the technological conditions of cinema) and moral.

Lisbon Story, a picaresque comedy which reprises the history of cinematic forms, has a far simpler narrative trajectory than *The End of Violence*, which attempts to combine at least three distinct story lines. It is a film which, like its immediate predecessor, is concerned with image contamination and the abuse of image technologies. Wenders also revisits some of his earlier preoccupations with the negative effect of the Hollywood cinema industry, particularly the proliferation of action movies with violent themes. The location is America, for the first time since 1984, this time the city of Los Angeles, the capital of the image industry and long associated with cultures of violence.

The theme of this film and its challenging, provocative title guaranteed it extensive media attention. It was widely and, for the most part, well reviewed and Wenders was interviewed in a range of newspapers and magazines where he spoke of his distaste for the use of violence in so much contemporary cinema. I think that the issue that "hooked" the media and secured the widespread attention is something of a red herring. I say this because although we are now at the end of a century of violence, in the longer historical view the contemporary situation in the "developed" world has seen the visible reduction and practical removal of various forms of violence from civil society, yet this has coincided with the heightened media visibility and sensuous/cultural appreciation of simulated or virtual violence. For most of the twentieth century also, violence (and sex) has been the most controversial emotive aspect of films and, later, television. This tended to peak at certain times. In the early 1990s, violence in Hollywood films aroused a lot of passions, especially films by Tarantino and Oliver Stone. There was, and is, talk of censorship and litigation. One case in point is the stance of John Grisham who called for a general boycott of films like *Natural Born Killers*, as well as a lawsuit against Stone which would seek to prove a causal link between the film and the death of a man called Bill Savage. His hope was that such litigation might become contagious. That particular lawsuit did not materialise, but a civil case brought by the relatives of a woman called Patsy Byers was allowed by the Supreme Court to go to trial.

Grisham's position was not untypical of a particular set of attitudes at that moment. The moment seems to have passed, and the BBC and Channel Four (a commercial UK television channel) have shown all the films which produced the controversy. *The End of Violence* was made (for a comparatively low budget of $5 million and in a relatively short time) in the context of these debates, but arguably it addresses far more important themes than Hollywood violence—issues of power, ownership, inequality, child abuse and the state's monopoly of the physical forces of violence. One target certainly is the uninterrogated and trivialised violence of the kind of films produced by Mike Max (*Creative Killing, Uncertain Death* and *The Seeds of Violence*) and gangsta rap in this film, but, as I have said, while screen violence has been the focus of the media attention it is peripheral to the film. As a theme it is even mocked in the highly stylised caricatures of "underclass" hired killers. The films of Tarantino, for example, with their   reflexive,   interrogative   qualities   and   their technical/representational scepticism, are not an issue.

So what are the issues? Wenders has this to say: "It's certainly not a film that deals with violence in a message sort of way . . . We chose the subject, but LA itself suggested it: the air is rich with the fear of violence in every form. In wealthy areas there's not a single house not connected to a surveillance system, with the Armed Response sign at the gate that says you'll be shot at if you enter" (quoted in Horton, 1997: 5).

The first issue is, therefore, a deeply structured inequality which gives rise to paranoia and talks up violence—or, rather, particular forms of violence—in class and ethnic terms. These are the same class and ethnic categories of people which service the global cities —the Hispanic cooks, gardeners and cleaners who offer Mike Max sanctuary after an attempt to kidnap him fails and he finds himself the subject of a murder hunt and becomes involved in a plot that may have come from one of his own movies. The focus on media violence, with its attention-grabbing headlines, is arguably a way of screening (in all senses of the word) and displacing the deeper kinds of violence, and while Wenders uses Max's formulaic action movies as a critical, and satirical, starting point, more sinister forms of violence are given increasing prominence. The link between these forms and Max's crude productions is somewhat naively articulated and, in the end, becomes little more than a means of bringing together the two young people— the stuntwoman-turned-actress Cat and the detective Doc Block—who, like Winter and Teresa in *Lisbon Story,* offer a way through to a possible future based upon an unmanipulative, shared love relationship brokered and protected by a young black female poet whose work speaks of abuse and violence.

Los Angeles is a global city, dominated by an interlocking and intersecting freeway culture which the film places and displaces. It is also what has been called an informational city—a space of flows, speed and compression, dehistoricized and culturally rootless. The informational city is characterised by image generation and highly advanced electronic technologies. Wenders has been described as anti-technological, and some of his 1980s comments tended in this direction, but the spaces in the film which suggest this—the residual humanism of the book-cluttered room of Ray Bering's father, the manual typewriter, the Hopperesque set of the film within a film and its heroine, and Ray's appearance and reappearance as a walking man with rucksack and staff—are there to slow down the flows, to check and interrogate the speed, suggesting a different pace and place (place-based social meaning) to contextualise and question not the technology itself but its uses and abuses. Ray, after all, uses e-mail and is half in love with the images and the machines he watches over in the Griffith Park Observatory; the "reformed" Mike Max returns to his house to retrieve his Psion organiser. So this is not Luddism (but note in the credits how Wenders is at pains to point out that all the editing has been done on film with traditional equipment) but an attempt to frame technology within an ethical imperative which is based upon concern for others, to create a space in which the possibility to act on the promptings of moral responsibility must be salvaged, or recovered, or made anew. This responsibility must exchange its now invalidated or forgotten priority for the superiority over technical-instrumental calculations. Salvaging the moral and the role of cultural technologies is at the heart of most of Wenders's 1990s output.

Initially, we see Mike Max centre stage, the focus of every shot, and calling the shots: the image producer and power-broker with the latest technology at his command—corporate, fast-talking, designer-clothed, utterly unreflexive, and living in sedentary luxury in Malibu. All experience is heavily mediated, distanced and emotionless; he communicates with his wife, Paige, only yards away, by portable phone. Resigned to no longer being able to command his attention, she tells him that she is leaving and going to do volunteer work in Guatemala. After a 400-page FBI file is dumped in his e-mail his life is transformed utterly, and the trauma of kidnapping leads him to vacate the centres of his yuppie life and head for the edges of society where he becomes, effectively, a spy and witness of his former life, an outcast and outsider. He shifts dramatically in his discourse, dress codes and mobility to become nomadic and peripheral—the man on the margins, marching to a different drum, living through the disintegrating, unmediated experience of persecution, obsession and paranoia. Paige decides not to leave for Guatemala but remains in their Malibu beach house and takes over the production company in Mike's absence, also linking up with the blaxploitation rap artist Six.

Ray Bering is also an image-processor, a NASA scientist conscripted to civil duties. One man produces simulations of violence; the other seeks to decode its "real" instances virtually and to bring it all within the range of a scopic regime: the one-way look of surveillance. The very phrase, " the end of violence as we know it," used by Ray's boss, echoes the phrase "the end of civilization as we know it." The very echo reminds us that there is no civilization, as we choose to define it, without its infrastructure of violence and barbarism. As has been said, the civilizing process is not about the uprooting but about *the redistribution of violence*. For me, this is the core of the film's meanings. The top-secret government surveillance technologies seek to extend the state's monopoly of violence in the name of ending it. This is made evident by the links made in the film with Guatemala and San Salvador, whose death squads are by no means solely indigenous but are linked to U.S. violence. Ray's cleaner, Matilda, a Guatemalan woman whose family was wiped out by the death squads and is in thrall to the FBI, is party to his assassination for leaking the file to Mike; even though they are in love, she is compelled by her role as agent (the life of her child is conditional upon this role) to sacrifice him. The scars on Matilda's body which Ray discovers/uncovers, are not simply physical but signs of her "enslavement" by the FBI. The absence of love is one of the many definitions of violence developed in the film, but Matilda's violence and love are nested in a set of impossible contradictions. Mike's conversation at the harbour with Matilda's child, as they look west away from America and towards the east, is, like the love of Cat and Doc, one of the markers of hope and of the future, the possibility of change and of salvaging value.

The End of Violence needs to be seen in the context of the post-1989 films of Wenders which all seem to be motivated by a form of politics (life-politics, perhaps, in the sense this is used by Giddens) centred on the ethical. The two central male figures are on a journey shaped around the problematic of seeing, in the literal sense of observation and visualisation, and in a cognitive and moral sense. Both men give up, walk away from forms of mastery, based upon the controlling look, the master/slave and subject/object relationship. Each becomes a meditative and reflexive witness in a post-Cold War world, a figure of revaluation and revision (hence the unusual shots of Los Angeles in its original desert and canyon landscape setting, and not just as the global city). Ray recognises that there is a landscape beyond the urban grid of LA, but its presence is obscured by pollution; the reference, the recognition, is also metaphorical. The film works with the possibility of becoming another, other than whom you are, a stranger confronting the otherness in ourselves, the very source of the ethical. That need, which is also a responsibility, for the other is paradoxically created by an assault, a breaking in upon the self. Max becomes a fugitive from his former self: "I became the enemy, and when the enemy I expected finally came they set me free." He hands his half of the company's proceeds (the proceeds of violence) to Ramon Gomez, his gardener, and his family (the victims of racism and violence). This ethical paradox seems to be the primary theme of the post-1989 films, where responsibility is lived as *election*, as choice, driven by a logic other than egologic.

The *hommage* shots of the planetarium dome of the Griffith Observatory refer to its use by Nicholas Ray in *Rebel Without A Cause*. Mike Max's dress is a conflation of James Dean's letterman jacket and Travis's clothing in *Paris, Texas*. The use of the Griffith is not a simple homage because, arguably, what Wenders is trying to present is two rebels *with* a cause, but one which the film does not labour to make overexplicit. The film works with a range of styles and genres—the names and action are cartoon-like in their two-dimensionality at times—but they often relate to each other discordantly. The standard critical response has been that this is a weakness, and in conventional terms it is, but what Wenders tried to do throughout the 1990s was to interrogate, subvert and unsettle many of the taken-for granted paradigms of western film-making, to expose them (in the filmic sense also) as overcodified and mediated to the point of cliché and platitude, rigid and lacking in innovation. Unlike a number of contemporary films (e.g., *Titanic*) this film is not "in your face" or "wall to wall", but leaves us as audience with lots of space in which to reflect and create meanings. Part of its strength lies in its place-based shots, the long and slow takes which shift the speeded-up rhythms of the city to a more measured and reflective pace, and the understated quality of both image and performance. This gives the violence another inflection altogether; it is not imaged, but its latency means we have to *imagine* it for ourselves and make the necessary connections. We are, in other words, the real detectives. In the context of a possible love, the violence perpetrated becomes more sinister and horrific, as we are made aware of the violated bodies and "enslaved" actions of those without election, without space to choose. It does end, however, with another possibility, another speculation, look and perspective: "I can see China now," Mike says to Matilda's child as they look out across the harbour; "I hope they can see us."

Wenders's recent film, *The Buena Vista Social Club* (1999) turns away from the United States and Europe and towards a small country which has been subjected to forty years of economic and cultural sanctions by the US: Cuba. In an interview in 1991, Wenders was asked whether he saw film-making as an archival activity, and he replied that this was unquestionably the case, a registering of that which was under threat, forgotten, or about to disappear. Unusually, he went on to say that he considered that feature films, with their "archival" locations, are the truly important documentaries of our time (Wenders, 1997: 133). *The Buena Vista Social Club* is not a feature film but an actual documentary which retrieves and recovers a lost performance tradition in Cuban music. The film was partly produced as a response to the phenomenal success of the million-selling, Grammy–award-winning CD of the same name. Ry Cooder, a major figure in postwar popular music often associated with Wenders's films, produced the CD and brought the musicians together for the recording sessions and concerts which the film focuses upon. The film has been almost as successful as the CD, playing to huge audiences in Britain and the United States, and was nominated both for a Golden Globe award and an Oscar. It was in the top ten of highest-grossing documentaries ever made before it was even released in Britain.

Cooder and Wenders have excavated the remains of a lost, but living, tradition and produced a work of cultural archaeology. Despite the fact that the Buena Vista Club closed more or less at the time when the Batista regime ended, the musicians did not leave for Miami, although some of them ceased to perform for many years. What Cooder felt he had recovered was "artistry and music that is nothing to do with money. It is not a money-based, power-based culture. Everybody feels connected to something humanistic and that's very hard to achieve. What can you look at that isn't saturated with commerce" (*The Guardian*, 1999: 2). Some reviewers have seen the film as anti-communist, others as soft on Castro and Cuba, but the film is rarely politically explicit, leaving comment to the look and sound of the film, to the music which Wenders has described as a form of nourishment.

The film is not just a documentary but also a work of oral history, recording and preserving the insights and memories of a range of musicians (from their late fifties to their nineties) whose voices and sounds have long been forgotten and, in some cases, will not survive for much longer. Revival and survival are celebrated by the film with its musical journey through the heart of Cuba, its provinces and regions as well as Havana, the capital. The Carnegie Hall concert given by the musicians (with tickets apparently being sold on the streets for $2,000) frames the film, forming its prelude and conclusion. The intervening period creates an uncondescending narrative space for the aging and forgotten, a showcase for skills, talents and authentic sounds. The scenes in New York towards the end of the film are patronising at times, partly because the men appear child-like in the context of western materialist culture, but the energy and vivacity of both the performances and the oral testimonies also give a sense, by analogy, of the "ontological gaze" which Wenders has always seen as the property of children. One of the most powerful scenes matches the beauty and grace of the child dancers and gymnasts with the extraordinary piano playing of the eighty-year-old Ruben Gonzalez. The palatial setting (a pre-Castro era casino) of their respective performances is very much shared space, intergenerational, linked through mutual rhythm and skill. Perhaps some of the impact of the film has been due to this physical and spiritual energy which an overmaterialist west would like to be able to see and feel with.

Although the film concentrates upon the contemporary presence of the musicians, there is a careful tracing of both individual and collective pasts combined with a dwelling on the origin of particular sounds and instruments with their local belongings and histories. One sequence focuses on the *laud*, an instrument which, with its Arabic and Spanish roots, was brought to Cuba by medieval troubadours. Time and again, the film emphasises this dimensionality and the need to historicise and mediate the narrative of the present, a break with sound-bites and image-selling which Wenders has long criticised. There is a strong sense of skills developed over time, of apprenticeship and respect, and of a different pace and rhythm. The singer Ibrahim Ferrer, in measured, almost formal tones, places this sense of performance as something achieved through and over time by saying that if they had followed the way of possessions they would have disappeared a long time ago. His narrative, which is characterised by its reference to a cultural and spiritual continuity carried by an African legacy, is a story of quiet resistance and persistence. He carries with him everywhere a Yoruba staff with its figure of Lazarus, the one who helps the disempowered. His songs stress place, the identity and sound of the deeply local.

The film is very much about grounding, about a Cuba of the back streets and side streets, the spaces hidden from the tourist eye. The Spanish architectural splendours are shown as fading, the cars are often 1950s Cadillacs and Buicks, but there is light, vibrant colour and the profound sense of an interactive popular culture. It is a work of tribute and respect, not only to the musicians themselves but to the people and culture that sustained them even in their absence. The film does not seek location shots merely as local colour but to give depth, context and perspective to the performances themselves. The musicians may be celebrated but they are not celebrities in the western sense, dislocated from place and community. Relationships are explored, not just stars. The powerful sense of the *ensemble* and the collective which is present throughout the film is not just produced by the foregrounded musicians but by the image continuum which embraces space, time and community. The Buena Vista is the catalyst and medium for this ensemble which is a work of anamnesis, a bringing into consciousness of heritage and history. The Cuban flag unfurled in Carnegie Hall was both an act of defiance and a sign of healing, a marker of a possible future. The concert brings together different cultural traditions and a range of performance styles, and reaches across generations. The concert, and indeed the whole film, resembles an intense and ongoing *conversation* of rhythm, sounds and personalities which, together, create an act of transcendence, a going beyond the immediate moment of performance.

In their different ways, all of Wenders's 1990s films have been about love, images and seeing. They are works of revaluation, of reconciliation and of healing. Each one is concerned with carving out space and time for the exploration of ethical practice and the possibilities of redemptive storytelling. Although Wenders has said that he considers that stories reaffirm the individuals' capacity to determine their own lives, the evidence of all the recent films suggests that it is narratives which are produced out of concerted action, ensemble practices, which offer the conditions of a future possibility. Creativity, imagination, love and filmmaking itself are all acts of cooperative endeavour. I am thinking of the Aboriginal people in *Until the End of the World*, the circus folk in *Faraway, So Close!*, the children and Madredeus in *Lisbon Story*, the Mexican-American gardeners in *The End of Violence* and, above all, the combined voices, instruments and memories of *The Buena Vista Social Club*. A complex network of mutualities, skills, and identities is established; in this last film, in particular, the vitality of the ensemble playing is a form of singing their world, their culture, into existence. The films come to inhabit a mode of intense and extended reflexivity. Each group of people performs an enabling function, making it possible to move beyond self-indulgent individualism, image saturation and the fixations of consumerism, towards a storying of hope and potential transformation—not changing the world, perhaps, but changing the images of the world.

Appendix: Filmography

SHORT FILMS

1967	*Locations (Schauplätze)*
1967	*Same Player Shoots Again*
1968	*Silver City*
1968	*Alabama: 2000 Light Years*
1969	*Polizeifilm*
1969	*3 American LP's (3 amerikanische LP's)*
1974	*Aus der Familie der Panzerechsen/Die Insel.*
1982	*Reverse Angle*
1982	*Chambre 666*
1992	*Arisha, the Bear and the Stone Ring*

FEATURE FILMS

1970	*Summer in the City: Dedicated to the Kinks*
1971	*The Goalkeeper's Fear of the Penalty (Die Angst des Tormanns beim Elfmeter)*
1972	*The Scarlet Letter (Der scharlachrote Buchstabe)*
1974	*Alice in the Cities(Alice in den Städten)*
1975	*Wrong Movement (Falsche Bewegung)*
1976	*Kings of the Road (Im Lauf der Zeit)*
1977	*The American Friend (Der amerikanische Freund)*
1980	*Lightning over Water (Nick's Film)*
1982	*Hammett*
1982	*The State of Things (Der Stand der Dinge)*

1984   *Paris, Texas*
1985   *Tokyo—Ga*
1987   *Wings of Desire (Der Himmel über Berlin)*
1989   *Notebooks on Clothes and Cities (Aufzeichungen zu Kleidern und Stadten)*
1991   *Until the End of the World (Bis ans Ende der Welt)*
1993   *Faraway, So Close! (In weiter Ferne, so nah!)*
1994   *Lisbon Story*
1995   *Beyond the Clouds (Par-Delà les Nuages)*
1996   *A Trick of the Light (Die Gebruder Skladanowsky)*
1997   *The End of Violence*
1999   *Buena Vista Social Club*
2000   *Million Dollar Hotel*

Bibliography

Adorno, T. *Minima Moralia*. London: NLB, 1974.

Andrews, G. *Time Out* , 29 June-6July 1994.

Bauman, Z. *PostModern Ethics*. Oxford: Blackwell, 1993.

Beck, U. *Risk Society: Towards a New Modernity*. London: Sage, 1992.

Benjamin, W. *Illuminations*. London:Collins/Fontana,1973.

Bhabha, H. *The Location of Culture*. London: Routledge, 1994.

Castells, M. *The Informational City*. Oxford: Blackwell, 1989.

Cixous, H. Fiction and Its Phantoms: A Reading of Freud's "The Uncanny." *New Literary History*, vol. 7, no. 3, Spring 1976.

Cohan, S., and I. R. Hark. *Screening the Male, Exploring Masculinities in Hollywood Cinema*. London: Routledge, 1993.

Cook, R., and G. Gemünden (eds.). *The Cinema of Wim Wenders: Image, Narrative and the Postmodern Condition*. Detroit: Wayne State University Press, 1997.

Cupitt, D. *What Is a Story?* London: SCM Press, 1991.

Dauman, A. *Pictures of a Producer*. London: BFI 1992.

Deleuze, G., and F. Guattari. *What is Philosophy?* London: Verso, 1994.

Eliade, M. *Shamanism: Archaic Techniques of Ecstasy*. London: Arkana, 1989.

Elsaesser, T. "Germany's Imaginary America: Wim Wenders and Peter Handke," in *European Cinema*, ed. S. Hayward. Birmingham: Modern Languages Department, Aston University, 1985.

Furman, N. "The Politics of Language: Beyond the Gender Principle," in *Making a Difference: Feminist Literary Criticism*, ed. G. Green and C. Kahn. London: Methuen, 1985.

Gallop, J. "The Mother Tongue," in *The Politics of Theory*, ed. Francis Barker et al. Colchester: University of Essex, 1983.

Gallop, J. *Reading Lacan*. Ithaca: Cornell University Press, 1985.

Gemünden, G. "I No Longer Trust the Narrative Power of Images: A Conversation with Wim Wenders." Unpublished interview, Berlin, March 1 1994.

Gregory, D. *Geographical Imaginations*. Oxford: Blackwell, 1994.

Harvey, D. *The Condition of PostModernity*. Oxford: Blackwell, 1989.

Highsmith, P. *Ripley's Game*. London: Penguin, 1974.

Horton, R. "Wim Wenders on the Road Again." *Film Comment*, March/April 1997.

Howarth, D. "Reflections on the Politics of Space and Time." *Angelaki*, vol. 1, no. 1, 1993, 52.

The Independent. 2 January 1997.

Kolker, R. P., and P. Beicken: *The Films of Wim Wenders: Cinema as Vision and Desire*. Cambridge: Cambridge University Press, 1993.

Kristeva, J. *Desire in Language*, ed. L. S. Roudiez. Oxford: Blackwell, 1980.

Kristeva, J. *Powers of Horror: An Essay in Abjection*, trans. L. S. Roudiez. New York: Columbia University Press, 1982.

Kristeva, J. *Revolution in Poetic Language*, trans. M. Waller. New York: Columbia University Press, 1984

Kristeva, J. "Stabat Mater," in *The Kristeva Reader*, ed. Toril Moi. Oxford: Blackwell 1987.

Kristeva, J. *Strangers to Ourselves*, trans. L. S. Roudiez. Hemel Hempstead: Harvester Wheatsheaf, 1991.

Kristeva, J. "Roman noir et temps present." *L'Infini* 37, Spring 1992.

Lash, S., and J. Urry. *Economies of Signs and Space*. London: Sage1994.

LeGates, R.T., and F. Stout (eds.). *The City Reader*. London: Routledge, 1996.

McAfee, N. "Abject Strangers: Toward an Ethics of Respect," in *Ethics, Politics, and Difference in Julia Kristeva's Writing*, ed. Kelly Oliver. London: Routledge, 1993.

Martin, B., and C. Mohanty. "Feminist Politics: What's Home Got to Do With It?" in *Feminist Studies/ Critical Studies*, ed. Teresa de Lauretis. London: Macmillan, 1988.

Nora, P. "Between Memory and History: *Les lieux de memoire*." *Representations*, no. 26, Spring 1989.

Paglia, C. *Sex and Violence, or Nature and Art*. London: Penguin, 1995.

Papastergiadis, N. *Modernity as Exile: The Stranger in John Berger's Writing*. Manchester: Manchester University Press, 1993.

Readings, B. *Introducing Lyotard: Art and Politics*. London: Routledge 1991.

Rosaldo, R. *Culture and Truth*. Boston: Beacon Books, 1989.

Rutherford, J. *Men's Silences*. London: Routledge, 1992.

Sanday, P. R. Female *Power and Male Dominance*. Cambridge: Cambridge University Press, 1981.

Sandford, J. *The New German Cinema*. New York: De Capo, 1980.

Schutz, A. *Collected Papers*, vol. 2. The Hague: Martinus Nijhoff, 1964.

Seidler, V. *Unreasonable Men*. London: Routledge, 1994.

Shephard, S. and W. Wenders: *Paris, Texas,* Screenplay, 21 September 1983 (unpublished).

Simmel, G. "The Stranger," in ed. K. H. Wolff . *The Sociology of Georg Simmel*, New York: Free Press, 1950.

Sontag, S. *On Photography*. London: Penguin, 1979.

Taylor, M. C. *Altarity*. Chicago: Chicago University Press, 1987.

Webster, D. *Looka Yonder*. London: Routledge, 1988.

Wenders, W. *Emotion Pictures*. London: Faber, 1989.

Wenders, W. *The Logic of Images*. London: Faber, 1991.

Wenders, W. *The Act of Seeing: Essays and Conversations*. London: Faber, 1997.

Winnicott, D. W. *Playing and Reality*. London: Penguin, 1988.

Index

About the Author

ROGER BROMLEY is Professor in International Cultural Studies and Director of the School of Graduate Studies and Research at Nottingham Trent University. He is the author of *Lost Narratives* and *Narratives for a New Belonging*.